WILD ALCHEMY

First published in Great Britain in 2024 by
Laurence King, an imprint of The Orion
Publishing Group Ltd, Carmelite House,
50 Victoria Embankment, London EC4Y 0DZ

An Hachette UK Company

10 9 8 7 6 5 4 3 2 1

Text © 2024 Jemma Foster
Illustrations © 2024 Andreas Brooks (openers)
Illustrations © 2023, 2024 Raxenne Maniquiz
(plants)

A CIP catalogue record for this book is available
from the British Library.

ISBN (Hardback) 978 0 857829153
ISBN (eBook) 978 1 399622134

Project Editor: Zoe Antoniou
Designer: Masumi Briozzo

Origination by F1 Colour Ltd
Printed in Dubai by Oriental Press

www.laurenceking.com
www.orionbooks.co.uk

CAUTIONS AND CONTRAINDICATIONS

This book and its remedies are intended to supplement, not replace, medical advice. If you know, or suspect, that you have a health problem, this should be examined and treated by a trained health professional.

Wild plants can cause allergic reactions. If you have known plant allergies, avoid all plants within that botanical family. Even if you have no known allergies, test remedies before use to check for sensitivities.

Apply a few drops on the tongue for internal remedies to test for an allergic reaction. Perform a patch test for external remedies by applying a small amount to the skin 24 hours before use. If any reaction occurs, do not use the remedy. When you take your first real dose, take the minimum amount initially and build up gradually if required.

If you are pregnant, lactating, trying to conceive or taking any medications, seek the advice of a trained health professional before taking any herbal remedies. Herbal medicines can react and interfere with pharmaceutical drugs, even common medicines such as the contraceptive pill and antidepressants.

The very young and very old should treat herbs with caution, and children under the age of two should not take herbal medicines unless under professional guidance. The remedies and dosages in this book are designed for adult usage. Some of the common contraindications are listed in this book, but it is by no means an exhaustive list.

The author and publisher specifically disclaim any liability, loss or risk, personal or otherwise, that is incurred as a consequence, directly or indirectly, of the use and application of any of the contents of this book.

Jemma Foster

WILD ALCHEMY

AN ASTRO-BOTANICAL GUIDE
TO THE MAGIC, MYTH
AND MEDICINE OF PLANTS

LAURENCE KING

Contents

Daisy (*Bellis perennis*).

THE ROSE OF VENUS

The orbital path of Venus around the Sun, from the perspective
of Earth, forming a five-petalled rose over an eight-year period.

Introduction

Alchemy is an ancient art of enquiry and transmutation working in symbiosis with the universal laws of nature. The laboratory of the alchemist is sacred, and, as with indigenous technologies, its practice is in communion with the spirits of nature and the elemental and cosmic forces guiding them. Alchemy is a system of relationships – of connection and correspondence, and of cause and effect – that considers the whole embrace of our experience.

The axiom 'As above, so below, as within, so without' describes the macro-microcosmic vision that is central to alchemical philosophy – that all universal phenomena correspond and relate to one another. It is through experiencing this oneness of being that we might diffuse the myth of separation and restore our fractured relationship to our planet.

A rose does not exist in isolation. From seed to bloom, it is in conversation with the elements that make up its physical reality, from the dance of the planets and the cycle of the seasons, to the Sun that feeds it light and the Moon that sets its rhythms. Just as we are influenced by the movements of the planets and stars above, so are plants guided in their development and expression. These correspondences are mirrored in the geometry cast by the orbit of the planets and the growth patterns of plants.

Alchemical philosophy is concerned with the *anima mundi* – the world soul that exists within all living beings. Its practice is to work with the existence of this soul within matter, and to transform matter into its original exalted form, integrating the spirit of the heavens into the physical realm. It is the sacred marriage of spirit and soul giving birth to spiritualized matter – the transmutation of the lead weight of our experience into celestial gold.

During the Age of Enlightenment and rise of Cartesian dualism, soul was separated from matter, and spirit from practice. The Gaian realms of elemental forces, nature spirits and more-than-human intelligence were externalized and disembodied from the whole. Earth was to be weighed, measured and contained. Symbiotic exchange was replaced with a system of rational abstract entities, of objectification and reductionism, and a shift was made from a three-dimensional to a two-dimensional lens where nature became the Other, something to be harnessed and tamed, setting the precedent for the Industrial Revolution and the colonization of natural resources in pursuit of unregulated growth. Truth was only sought through extraction and isolation. Alchemy became corrupted with the manipulation and exploitation of nature for personal gain, and people sought its wisdom solely in pursuit of gold. These lower alchemists were called 'puffers', toiling away at their bellows, deaf to the voice of spirit. And because of this, their efforts were futile. The true nature of alchemy became enshrouded in complex symbolism only available to discerning initiates, and was forced into the occult as chemistry was born.

Our disconnection from nature has become institutionalized and culturally ingrained. Nature is exploited, appropriated and measured, and person–plant relations are filed under myth and folklore. However, as nature is us, we are it. And the yearning for that resonance to return is a desire for wholeness that exists within each of us. This book is a calling to reclaim our true nature and fertilize the soils of our individual and collective future. It is an invitation to reposition ourselves away from the anthropocentric perspective and become entangled with other beings, forming co-creative partnerships with the more-than-human and shifting the lens from resource to relationship. Through embodied philosophy and practice, we might connect back to ourselves, to our roots and to the wild, and in doing so, to our intuitive and feeling selves as we begin to listen from the intelligence of the heart. In reuniting our inner and outer worlds, we enter into a coherent state of being, where we are open to receiving this wisdom. Plants are our true ancestors, credited for our evolution and continued existence. These masters of adaption and survival can be our greatest teachers, if we only learn to listen.

How to Use This Book

.

Wild Alchemy is written for anyone who wants to cultivate a relationship with the environment, nature, the cosmos and themselves. You may be a herbalist wanting to integrate astrology into your practice; an astrologer wanting to explore herbalism; a forager or gardener wanting to work with the cycles and rhythms of the planets; or simply a lover of the wild who wants to bring the magic of plants into your daily life through remedy-making. In essence, we are all born alchemists, and this is just an opportunity to awaken the wisdom within.

This book is intended to introduce you to the concepts of botany, wildcrafting, cultivation and traditional herbal remedies through the lens of astrology and alchemy. The plants listed in this book primarily exist in the wild and can be sourced directly, and are predominantly native to the Northern Hemisphere, although some more exotic plants and culinary herbs and spices, such as ginger, turmeric and saffron, have also been included. Advocating for diversity in plants and believing that there is no such thing as a 'weed', I have included some plants that are undervalued or overlooked. Pineappleweed is an example of this – resilient and determined, it can be found pushing through the cracks in the pavement.

There are many ways in which we can receive the benefits of a plant, from the physical (ingestion of food and medicine, or topical applications of creams, oil infusions and high-frequency essential oils) to the vibrational (direct perception and meditation, and flower essences which rely on the memory of water to hold the vibrational signature of the plant). In alchemical preparations, we always consider the vibrational aspect of a remedy and how these subtle elements can influence different aspects of healing. It is not just the physical body that plants can heal; they can also be used to treat emotional conditions, such as grief or sadness, and mental issues such as anxiety or poor memory. Flower essences are a key ally, as they act upon the emotional and mental body, opening up pathways to deeper healing. Plants are used for many magical purposes, such as in spells and rituals, in incense and amulets.

Our journey along the transformational path begins with the principles of Alchemical Cosmology and Philosophy in chapter 1, and the role of astrology within it. We will learn about how all alchemical processes are rooted in the internal transformation of the alchemist. We will bring this wisdom into the wild in chapter 2 with Plant Communication, Wildcrafting and Botany, and establish methods of identification, harvesting and cultivating plant allyships through effective conversation. Here, you can refer to the section on Wildcrafting (see page 28) for ethical foraging practices. In chapter 3, The Alchemy of Plants, Planets and People, we will investigate the sensory perception of plant chemistry, and what morphology and habitat reveals about a plant. We will navigate the relevance of timing, such as when to plant and harvest in relation to the cycles of the Moon, planetary days of the week and seasonality. We will also explore cultivation and the traditional physic (medicine) garden. In Astro-anatomy, we will look at elemental pathology and the role of the planets and the zodiac when it comes to influencing plants and people. Lastly, we will look at how all of this functions in the anatomy and physiology of the body.

At the core of the book is chapter 4, The Alchemical Herbal, which covers the plants and remedies that correspond to the elements, planets and signs of the zodiac. This system looks at plants through a specifically elemental and astrological lens, but can also be used as a traditional A–Z by referring to the Index. You may also look up a particular plant, planet, zodiac sign, ailment or remedy in the Index and jump straight to your point of interest.

With this knowledge we go into chapter 5, The Laboratory, where we will learn how to set up our alchemical space and how to process and prepare plants. We'll also explore different methods of extraction and types of alchemical preparations, remedies and formulas. At the end of the book, you'll also find suggestions for further reading, and a glossary of terms.

Some of the content and practices in this book are complex and might appear overwhelming at first, but just start with what you feel most comfortable with or most compelled by. If you have no prior knowledge, begin with the elements (see page 54), as these are the building blocks of everything in existence and provide the foundation for understanding astrology. Then, explore body systems and elemental pathology (see pages 48–51) to see how the elements function in the body.

If you are new to astrology, begin with the cycles of the Moon, viewing the Moon at night to see the waxing and waning of its shape. On the new moon, make an intention for this cycle to come to fruition at the full moon – such as completing a creative or emotional task, like resolving an issue – and make notes of how you feel as the Moon moves through its phases. You might also want to look up your astrological chart based on your place and time of birth. Find out which of the zodiac signs your sun, moon and ascendant fall in, and consider how this relates to you. You can then incorporate this into your lunar practice by looking up the signs that the Moon moves through throughout the month as it passes through the zodiac, which changes every couple of days. Pay particular attention to when the Moon is in the same sign as it was when you were born.

If you are new to plants or herbalism, go for a walk in your local area and begin to notice the plants that grow there. Engage all your senses and notice any changes as the days go by; you may wish to document these, whether photographically, by drawing or by creating a herbarium (see page 31). You can follow the Plant Communication guide on page 24 to establish and build relationships with the plants.

You can immediately begin to work with any plant in this book energetically, either by following one of the visualizations or meditations (see pages 25–27) or by turning to a random page in The Alchemical Herbal; pick a plant, close your eyes and bring it into your field of awareness by holding its name or image in your mind, then receive it into your heart.

A NOTE ON REMEDY-MAKING

The remedies in this book are largely based on a system of ratios. This supports a balanced approach to wildcrafting that allows you to fulfil the demands of a recipe, while also providing you with the formula for responsible harvesting, so that you can work out the remedy based on the amount of plant that has been picked and then engineer your remedy accordingly. The Laboratory chapter offers essential information that you can refer to when creating some of the remedies.

A NOTE OF CAUTION

Many herbs have a long tradition of safe and common usage. However, it is still possible for these plants to produce allergic reactions in some people, and particular care should be taken with wild plants that the body isn't accustomed to. General cautions are highlighted in the remedies, while key poisonous plants are referred to in the guidance on safe wildcrafting (see page 29) and further information on allergies is listed in the Plant Directory (see page 186).

Dog rose (*Rosa canina*).

CHAPTER I

ALCHEMICAL COSMOLOGY AND PHILOSOPHY

Alchemical Cosmology

In alchemical cosmology, the primordial creative void from which everything arises and passes into existence is known as *prima materia*, 'first matter'. It is the unity consciousness responsible for all of creation. In order to know itself, it separates into duality as celestial niter (the masculine, yang, upward, animating force), from which the first volatile and dynamic elements of air and fire are born, and then into celestial salt (the fundamental feminine form, yin, downward), from which the fixed, receptive elements of water and earth are produced. These are the universal principles of duality and correspondence – Sun and Moon, yin and yang, *anima* and *animus*, masculine and feminine, king and queen, spirit and soul. The fifth element, known as aether or quintessence, is the invisible vital force that gives life to the universe. It is an eternal light pulsing through all forms and beings, and the celestial monochord that gives harmony to the music of the spheres.

PRIMA MATERIA

The primary elements of earth, air, fire and water are further condensed and recombined into the *tria prima*, or 'three essentials', which are a primal trinity consisting of salt, mercury and sulphur.

TRIA PRIMA

FIRE + AIR = SULPHUR — SOUL-IGNITING FORCE

AIR + WATER = MERCURY — SPIRIT-MEDIATING FORCE

EARTH + WATER = SALT — BODY-INTEGRATING FORCE

PRIMA MATERIA

All life is seeded from this cosmic hinterland, beyond time and space, perceived by the alchemists as the unity consciousness or supramental mind known as One Mind. It is the source responsible for all of creation and from which is formed the *anima mundi* (world soul). The *prima materia* is perceived as the chaos state, and yet it is pure and infinite in potential, as all possibilities exist within it. Johann Wolfgang von Goethe once called architecture condensed light, and this is a way of perceiving physical reality: as light condensed into form. Out of the quantum field, waves collapse into particles and energy condenses, forming a vibrational interference pattern that crystallizes into physical form, as stars become fixed into leaves and flowers, flesh and bone.

In *De Anima* (*On the Soul*), Aristotle discusses this process of distillation into the physical realm as *entelecheia* (or 'entelechy'), meaning that which brings into reality what is otherwise merely potential. He distinguished matter as the elements of which an entity is composed, and form as the soul or vital formative force that makes a living organism and gives it function and purpose. In *Alchemy and Psychology* Carl Jung defines *prima materia* as the world soul captive within a grand cosmic egg (or 'Orphic Egg'). This is depicted with a serpent (named Ananke) wrapped around it. In the

PRIMA MATERIA

Celestial Salt   *Celestial Niter*

FIXED   VOLATILE

EARTH   WATER   AIR   FIRE

SALT   SULPHUR

MERCURY

Yggdrasil, the Mundane Tree, Baxter's Patent Oil Printing, from a plate included in the English translation of the Prose Edda *Northern Antiquities* by Oluf Olufsen Bagge (1847).

'The cosmos is within us. We are made of star-stuff. We are a way for the universe to know itself.'

CARL SAGAN

laboratory, this is the crucible, and it is the purpose of the alchemical process to liberate the soul from the matter it is contained within.

From the *prima materia* emerges a life that strives towards order, and towards a predestined condition based on the life force and boundary conditions guiding it, such as genetics. There is a self-organizing, fractal behaviour at play in this process of realization – from waves to particles, subatomic to atomic, atoms to molecules, to cells and systems. The body is an example of this, with trillions of cells harmonizing in a highly complex symphony of synchronization.

The union of heaven and earth, of the macrocosm and the microcosm, is symbolized by the *axis mundi* – the world axis or centre of the world, often depicted as a world tree, or the tree of life. The concept of the world tree exists in many cultures, with the branches connecting the trunk of the earth to the celestial skies, and the roots reaching to the underworld. In Norse mythology, it is the mythical Yggdrasil, containing the nine realms of the cosmos.

In alchemical practice as we will see on page 17, the first process is death, as only then can the soul be released. It is necessary for the soul to return to the

prima materia in order to tap into its infinite potential and be restructured as something greater than itself. This continual cycle of birth, death and renewal and the transmigration of souls (reincarnation or palingenesis) is depicted in the ouroboros, an ancient symbol of a serpent eating its own tail. The practice of alchemy is a conduit of perfection. It is to work in unison with nature, to assist, to support and to quicken its desires. In alchemical terms, adaptation and evolution must happen on the spiritual, energetic plane in order to occur on the physical plane of reality.

TRIA PRIMA

In creation, mercury (the spirit) carries the soul (sulphur) into the body (salt). The body (matter) integrates both the soul (passion, desire) and the spirit (imagination, intellect), and embodies them into form, as energy condensed into thought forms into material reality. Mercury is the vital mediating force that integrates all the elements of the *tria prima*, because in its role of spirit it unites soul and matter. Mercury is likened to living light: the quantum shapeshifter that is both the masculine volatile waveform and the fixed feminine of particles. Spirit and soul are entwined in a dance which is fluid and dynamic. Note that in some later alchemical texts, this relationship was redefined, and mercury became the soul and sulphur the spirit.

The Great Work

The practical application of the wisdom of these universal forces in the transmutation and spiritualization of matter is described in The Great Work, or *Magnum Opus*. It is the process of harnessing the *prima materia* through the elemental forces in order to produce the Philosopher's Stone, the immortal elixir capable of giving life and immortality. It can be interpreted as both a physical and metaphysical practice. While Western alchemy originated from Egypt through the Greco-Roman empires, and before that the Chaldean, Phoenician and Babylonian civilisations, Eastern alchemy emerged independently from China, Tibet and India.

The Egyptian god Tehuti (Thoth), known as the 'Master of Masters' or the 'Scribe of the Gods', transcribed the universal order according to divine beings through the sacred arts, and taught humankind about the ways of the universe through writing, art, astrology, mathematics, music and sacred geometry. Thoth was traditionally represented with the head of an ibis and wearing a crescent moon. He became known to the Greeks as Hermes Trismegistus ('Thrice-Greatest Hermes') after Hermes Mercurius, the winged-messenger god, mediator between matter and soul, and Mercury, the trickster god of communication, trade and travel in Roman mythology. Healer and psychopomp, he was the guardian of souls. The established philosophical system based on the teachings of Hermes Trismegistus was considered to be the embodiment of the Universal mind, and is known as Hermeticism.

Hermeticism is rooted in an understanding of the interplay of universal elements and celestial objects, such as the luminaries (Sun and Moon), the planets of our solar system and the constellations of the zodiac. It engages with the mineral, plant, animal and fungi kingdoms, and invokes universal laws to transform them into medicine and magic. Any process requires a degree of purification of the alchemist on a physical, psychological and mental level. It is as much about the transformation of a substance as it is of the soul.

Hermes Trismegistus existed across time and space as the mediator between the *as above* of the spirit world and the *as below* of the material world. In Greco-Roman imagery, he carries the caduceus, a staff with two intertwining serpents which has come to represent medicine in modern symbolism. Some occult texts described the caduceus coil as an auric device that could alter the electromagnetic field of any living thing. It represents the masculine and feminine forces entwined, yin and yang, and the salt and the sulphur mediated by mercury, and bears a striking resemblance to the double helix.

A putto pours a phial into a dragon's mouth, pumping a bellows with his other hand; this represents the fixing of volatile matter in the alchemical process. Watercolour painting by E. A. Ibbs, 1900–1909, part of *Splendor Solis*.

The Emerald Tablet

The Emerald Tablet – also known as the Smaragdine Tablet – is a treatise on the mysteries of the universe. It describes the secret workings of nature and a universal pattern that is the blueprint for transformation across all planes of existence. It is thought to have been created by Thoth during what the ancient Egyptians called 'Zep Tepi', or 'First Time', around 12,000 years ago, when divine beings described as 'visitors from the firmament' came to Earth. Before the Great Flood, Thoth protected his teachings in one gold and one emerald pillar containing scrolls and a green crystalline tablet, then known as the 'Pillars of the Gods of the Dawning Light', and later as the 'Two Pillars of Hermes'. These are thought to have been discovered thousands of years later by the pharaoh Amenhotep IV (who later changed his name to Akhenaten, meaning 'he who serves the Sun'), who reformed his kingdom in light of their teachings, with the Operation of the Sun as the central creative force of the universe, but they were lost again when he was exiled as a heretic.

TABULA SMARAGDINA
Translation by Islamic alchemist, Jâbir ibn Ḥayyân (Geber):

Truth! Certainty! That in which there is no doubt!
That which is above is from that which is below, and that which is below is from that which is above, working the miracles of one.
As all things were from one.
Its father is the Sun and its mother the Moon.
The Earth carried it in her belly, and the wind nourished it in her belly, as earth which shall become fire. Feed the Earth from that which is subtle, with the greatest power.
It ascends from the Earth to the heaven and becomes ruler over that which is above and that which is below.

Alexander the Great once again unearthed the scrolls, which inspired the building of Alexandria, with the Emerald Tablet at its heart – and, for the first time, in public view. It was translated into Greek and studied by priests, academics and mystics. One of Alexandria's Hermeticists, Zosimus of Panopolis, determined the tablet to be a path towards spiritual evolution for the purification and perfection of the soul.

The seven fundamental Hermetic principles of the Emerald Tablet were interpreted in *The Kybalion* (1908) written mysteriously by 'Three Initiates':

> *1. Mentalism: The ALL is the MIND; the Universe is mental.*
> *2. Correspondence: As above, so below; as below, so above.*
> *3. Vibration: Nothing rests; everything moves; everything vibrates.*
> *4. Polarity: Everything is Dual; everything has poles; everything has its pair of opposites.*
> *5. Rhythm: Everything flows, out and in; everything has its tides; all things rise and fall.*
> *6. Cause and Effect: Every Cause has its Effect; every Effect has its Cause; everything happens according to Law.*
> *7. Gender: Gender is in everything; everything has its Masculine and Feminine Principles; Gender manifests on all planes.*

It should be noted that gender in alchemical philosophy does not refer to gender as we know it in modern times. This is an archetypal and symbolic concept that represents energies or qualities that exist within all of us.

Internal Alchemy

HEAL THYSELF

The path of the alchemist is also an inward journey of the transformation of the soul, shining light into the shadows and purifying the self of lower vibrational states. The psyche is represented by the alchemical *vas* (vessel) or crucible, which holds all opposing forces within. The psycho-spiritual alchemical journey begins with a process of letting go and culminates in the distillation and refinement of character that is able to function in a coherent state. It is the marriage of the conscious and unconscious mind, which Jung referred to in depth psychology as 'individuation'. There is so much noise in our modern world that creates dissonance, and when we take that, or our thoughts, into our practice or the natural world, we are vibrating at a chaotic frequency that is out of harmony with our environment. When we are in a coherent state, we resonate with our environment on the same frequency or wavelength to receive and exchange information. The crucible is like a chrysalis, holding all potential as it unfolds and transforms.

A path of initiation, alchemy requires the marriage of the intuitive, emotional lunar self, with the rational, thinking solar self into a cosmic-stellar self that speaks with the direct perception that the Egyptians called the 'intelligence of the heart'. Spiritual alchemy is either a practice in itself or it is the prerequisite to practical alchemy – any experiment in the laboratory requires the transformation of the inner crucible of the alchemist. Just as there is danger in quickening the flames in the laboratory, transformation of the psyche should also not be forced. Alchemy is concerned with a return to source, to the essence of our soul. If we want to enact change in the physical world, we also need to work on the spiritual or energetic planes. We must enact the changes we wish to see in the world within ourselves first. Visualize a prism: pure light (spirit or pure awareness) enters it, and is then refracted into the electromagnetic spectrum as a rainbow (physical reality). The quality and condition of the prism (us) determines the outcome.

The ultimate transmutation of the mind is through the dissolution of fixed thinking into a fluid motion where there is no space for rigid thinking, doctrine or polarization, opening up space for new paradigms and opportunities. We enter into a state of intuitive flux, guided by the rhythm and flow of cause and effect, holding us accountable for our actions and demanding that we consider the greater picture and the impact that each of our actions will have on the collective. The principle of polarity in alchemy teaches the reconciliation of seemingly opposed forces and that the tension between opposites is only a matter of degree. The nature of a force is the same: the crest and trough of the same wave are on a gradient scale. Light and dark, hot and cold, love and hate – at what point does one stop and the other end? The alchemical marriage symbolizes awakened consciousness through the reconciliation of opposing forces.

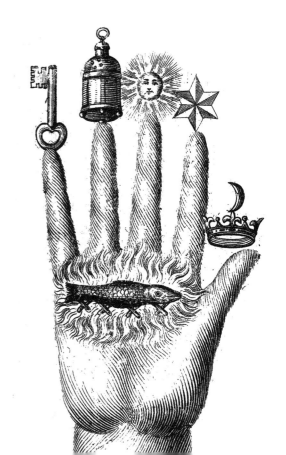

SOLVE ET COAGULA

Alchemical preparations, known as spagyrics in Latin, for 'purify by resolution', has its origins in the Greek *spao* ('to draw out' or 'tear apart') and *ageiro* ('to assemble'). Alchemy is a vibrational science which states that energy is transformed by altering the manifestation of a mass. This is achieved by deconstructing the existing state, separating its parts (*solve*) into its basic primary elements, to release the spirit and soul from the body, and releasing the pure vital energy stored within. Then, with this creative force, they are put back together again (*coagula*) into a new, exalted state. This need to erode and decay is a maturation process that evolves the material to its highest virtue. To build awareness of these subtle states, the path of the alchemist is first to cultivate our inner expansion and intuition – a psycho-spiritual practice of elevating the base elements of their experience to a noble state – and then to transform the leaden qualities that weigh down and limit life into the golden ones that lift up and expand our field of awareness. With this in mind, we can review the alchemical processes as a journey through the inner landscape of the alchemist.

'The opus magnum had two aims: the rescue of the human soul, and the salvation of the cosmos.'

CARL SAGAN

THE SEVEN OPERATIONS / SEVEN RAYS

Encoded within the Emerald Tablet, the alchemists extracted a formula for the practical applications of its seven principles, known as the 'Seven Operations' or 'Seven Rays', which were at once a physical and metaphysical process. Described here are the basic laboratory steps, along with the psycho-spiritual counterparts from a Jungian perspective to support inner growth.

1. Calcination: Heating a substance with fire to reduce to ashes (death of individual ego and collective super ego, lifting out of depression, bringing order out of chaos, burning off the dross).
2. Dissolution: Dissolving of ashes in water (dissolution of outdated belief systems, prejudices and rigidity of thinking, letting go).
3. Separation: Filtration of solution (the divided self, separation from reality in order to meet oneself objectively).
4. Conjunction: Reconstitution of elements of separation (union of opposites, sacred marriage, integration of archetypes, thinking and feeling unite).
5. Fermentation: Putrefaction of conjunction (dark night of the soul, meeting of shadow aspects, inspiration enters and a new level of consciousness filters through).
6. Distillation: Boiling and condensing of fermented solution (emergence of the transpersonal self and true nature).
7. Coagulation: Precipitation of distillation, releasing the *ultima materia* or supercelestial *arcanum* known as the Philosopher's Stone, from which the *elixir vitae* (elixir of life and immortality) can be formed (integration of transpersonal self into embodied experience).

Alchemical Practice

During the alchemical process of the Seven Operations or Seven Rays (see page 17), there are four primary phases: Nigredo (black, earth element), Albedo (white, air element), Citrinitas (yellow, water element) and Rubedo (red, fire element). During the Renaissance, the Citrinitas phase was absorbed into the Rubedo, creating a three-phase system. Dragons were considered to be carriers and protectors of the vital force and represented the uncontrollable desires and chaos potential of the universe that exist within each of us. Each operation was assigned a particular dragon archetype, and each phase required an exchange with the dragon forces held within the alchemist. Nigredo is *facing the dragon*, shining light on the shadow within. Albedo is *surrendering to the dragon*, with acceptance and an energy of letting go. Rubedo calls for *unleashing the dragon* though integration of new energies, transformation and transcendental power.

The Nigredo or blackening stage occurs during the first two stages of the alchemical process: calcination and dissolution. Transformation begins with letting go of the old, reduced to ashes through the fire of calcination. This serves to burn away crude impurities, leaving the most ethereal form so that it is only the fundamental essence that enters into the following stages. Calcination is the necessary death required for resurrection, like the phoenix that will eventually rise from the ashes. Its element is fire and its role is purification through the destruction of contaminants. Physically, this occurs through the digestive fire that assists in catabolic and metabolic processes and the elimination of toxins. This may mean mortal death, or it can be psycho-spiritual, through the destruction of limiting belief patterns, ego and hubris. This stage is symbolized by a black crow or raven, which represents a withdrawal from the external, sensory world into the inner world of the alchemist.

Through dissolution, the element of water washes the impurities away and signifies a return to the amniotic fluid of the womb and the chaos nature of the vast cosmic ocean. As the ashes are dissolved in water, so

too does the purified ego dissolve into our inner waters and the emotional body. Emotions rise up as energy and as vapour, condensing into liquid, and mirroring the weather system of our planet and Gaia. These emotions are then released through tears, dreams and visionary states. In the physical body, this can be supported through lymphatic cleansing, fasting and flushing out toxins through detoxification practices.

From the darkness comes the light, and the Albedo or whitening stage consists of separation and conjunction through the elements of air and earth. The new essence created during the Nigredo phase must now undergo further refinement and purification, first through separation – separating the subtle from the gross, and breaking down and dividing a substance to reveal its primary components through filtration and aeration. Separation is symbolized by a white goose or swan, representing the light of the soul filtering into the darkness. These dual forces within the essence are referred to as the king and queen. After the initial chaos of the destruction of ego aspects, this process allows the alchemist to see things as they truly are, and to establish what is necessary to leave behind and what remains. Through this, it is possible to witness the unborn self and identify the parts within that need to be cultivated. This is assisted in the body through breathwork, meditation and altered states of consciousness. Conjunction occurs through the earth element as the alchemical marriage of the king and queen, of solar and lunar forces, to produce a child. As detailed in the alchemical parable *The Alchemical Wedding of Christian Rosenkreutz*, this stage is symbolized by a rooster, reflecting a new virility.

All of the refined components that resulted from the separation process are now put back together in the conjunction, but not as they were – this is a new, purified, reborn earth element, and an integration of all the elements in their exalted states and the spiritualization of matter. This is a time of deep communion with the self to cultivate discernment, refinement and integration. This is often depicted in alchemical texts as a Rebis – a winged hermaphrodite with a male head on the right and a female head on the left.

In a final stage of purification, this new evolved form must also undergo a death through putrefaction known as fermentation. It is the final letting go of anything the egoic mind is holding on to and any residual impurities. This happens through a stage of incubation and gestation, when living cells or bacteria bring the dead matter of the previous stages to life through fermentation, which awakens and revitalizes the ego, breathing in new life. This stage of Citrinitas is the dawning of the solar light and the stirring of the light within the alchemist, which can be seen as spiritual forces or the new light of consciousness penetrating the soul, and the visions in the imaginal realm that alchemists called true imagination. From here, the peacock's tail emerges, symbolizing the dawn of a new day. Again, we see the way that pure white light enters into a prism and is refracted across the light spectrum as a rainbow. Similarly, the rainbow of the peacock's tail is a reflection of the new consciousness that is entering the substance. A milky white fluid appears as a sign of life emerging from the darkness, bringing clarity and insight. Here, we see the sulphur of the soul purified through the work, and united with mercury of the spirit to form the salt: the mother of the stone. The distillation process consists of multiple distillations occurring through the boiling and condensation of the solution to release its pure essence or spirit in the vapours, known as 'letting the eagles fly'. This is a spiralized process rather than a linear one, as it is recursive and fractal, occurring through many phases of the psyche and many lifetimes. Continued agitation and sublimation of psychic forces to remove impurities constantly works to elevate the subtle from the gross in a continued refinement of character. It is the spiritual fire that heats these parts, lights our desires and can trigger emotional reactions as a way of revealing our inner state.

Ultimately, this leads to the integration and alignment of energy centres in the body. Here, the alchemist must sacrifice the last of themselves in order to feed their newborn selves, represented by the pelican, which pierces its chest to feed its young with its own blood.

At last, the Sun rises with the final Rubedo phase, the (re)birth of the true self. Coagulation is the physical manifestation of the essence created during the conjunction – the crystallization of these forces into the Philosopher's Stone. The body is made spiritual and the soul is made corporeal. It is the spiritualization of matter and the materialization of spirit. This is the enlightened, transcendental self, and the sacred seed that lies dormant within us until it is awakened through experience and devotional practice. At this stage, the alchemist requires nothing and can transcend the material world. This is the Holy Grail. Its symbol is the phoenix: the resurrected personality, sometimes called Ortus, meaning 'rectified one' or the Hermes Bird. Swiss alchemist Paracelsus called this cosmic essence Illiaster, meaning 'star in man', and it is the *ultimate materia* of the soul.

ALCHEMICAL COSMOLOGY AND PHILOSOPHY   19

As Above, So Below

The practice of astrology is an alchemical opus in itself. Astrology is a dynamic system of relationships that provides a map for the alchemist. Knowledge of the planets and their cycles is intrinsic to alchemical practice. Astrology is deeply woven into the fabric of alchemical lore.

If we envision the universe as inherently holographic, and the *prima materia* as the infinite field of potential, it is from that place that the soul originates as pure light and awareness. This cosmic consciousness is condensed into the concentrated light of the astral body, which distils the soul into the body. Astrology comes from *aster*, meaning 'star' in Greek. The astral plane is the energetic field of the cosmos. At the moment of birth, these energetics collapse into a concentrated point, creating a blueprint for that person. The natal chart is hermetically sealed at birth; it is the energy matrix containing the past, present and future spiritual DNA of an individual at the moment that they take their first breath and incarnate into the physical world – the alchemical spiritualization of matter. Each planet diffuses a particular ray or electromagnetic frequency out into the solar system. This is received, absorbed or reflected by the other planetary forces, which then determine the specific energy or 'sidereal vapour' (from the Latin *sider*, meaning 'star') it emanates.

In the transmutation of base metals, lead, tin, iron and copper are melted and fused into a black alloy. When heated with silver and then with mercury (quicksilver), it becomes white, followed by an iridescent yellow-red-violet colour known as the peacock's tail, before finally turning gold. This transition from lead into gold was called the Ladder of the Planets, corresponding to the seven visible celestial bodies as 'planets' inclusive of the Sun and Moon. The ladder travels from the periphery of the solar system – cold, dark, distant Saturn, represented by lead – in towards the Sun, which represents not only the Sun of our solar system but also the esoteric concept of the Grand Central Sun and our

> ## 'Understand that the medicine must be prepared in the stars and that the stars become the medicine.'
>
> PARACELCUS

own inner sun: the true nature of the self that is pure, noble and with the perfection of gold. As alchemists, we engage in these transformational processes to turn the lead weight of our experience and lower consciousness into the gold of the enlightened soul and cultivate a greater state of awareness and connection. Applying the alchemical process to material life, working in unison with the cosmos, transforms the astrological chart into the Philosopher's Stone.

LADDER OF THE PLANETS	
GOLD/SUN	COAGULATION
SILVER/MOON	DISTILLATION
QUICKSILVER/MERCURY	FERMENTATION
COPPER/VENUS	CONJUNCTION
IRON/MARS	SEPARATION
TIN/JUPITER	DISSOLUTION
LEAD/SATURN	CALCINATION

The Philosopher's Stone

The Philosopher's Stone – or *lapis* – is achieved through the accumulation, purification and perfection of the *prima materia*. It is often represented by the Hermetic Seal of Light (above), which is symbolic of quintessence and the synthesis of body, spirit and soul. Adulterated by the gross states of material form manifesting in the lower earthly realms, it must first be sought out within matter, extracted and then applied with purpose to breathe life into an object or state of being. It is then used to bring dead matter, or chemical compounds, alive with the breath of the divine. Some alchemists believe that the stone is carbon in all its potential, and the gatekeeper between worlds that brings cosmic creations into shape and form. If the *prima materia* is effectively harnessed and purified, it becomes the Philosopher's Stone, from which anything can be given life. Once the Philosopher's Stone has been achieved, projection and multiplication can then occur. Projection allows for the redemption of matter and the transmutation of the base into the spiritual, turning lead into gold. Multiplication allows the results of these processes to be multiplied and increased in potency.

If the Philosopher's Stone is an immortal elixir that animates and gives life where there is degeneration or decay – allowing one to live with vitality and longevity without craving or attachment – then it is the same as that which many esoteric traditions describe as the accomplishment of the spiritual path: the attainment of enlightenment and the liberation of the soul. The Philosopher's Stone is planet Earth, Gaia, in her archetypal form as a return to unity consciousness.

Scientist and environmentalist James Lovelock proposed the Gaia hypothesis that all living organisms form a synergetic and self-regulating system to maintain homeostasis of the planet. 'Daisyworld' is a hypothetical planet where only black and white daisies exist, regulating the temperature of the planet by absorbing or reflecting sunlight. Here we see the harmony of opposites and how equal opposing forces can work together to create equilibrium when in balance. This is also true of our

internal alchemy, or our conscious and unconscious, light and shadow forces. The two must exist together. The journey of the soul transforms the shadow through acceptance rather than rejection, to work as a whole.

As human consciousness exists in Jung's collective unconscious, so too does that of plants and more-than-human intelligence. Rupert Sheldrake's theory of morphic resonance demonstrates the inherited memory of all living organisms, and suggests an innate knowledge and sharing of information that exists in the unseen fields of awareness. Plants, like us, exist in the liminal: the numinous, mythical land of dreams and altered states where worlds exist within worlds, known as the *mundus imaginalis*. It is here, as is the practice in many indigenous cultures, that we may converse and divine with plant spirits. Culturally, we have become left-brain dominant (stuck in the analytical and logical), and in order to tip the pendulum, we need to embrace more of the right brain (the creative, intuitive and sensing side). Ultimately, we need both working in sync and cooperating.

An understanding of the subtle energetics of life informed the practices of our ancestors, instructing the planting, cultivation and harvesting of crops, ceremony and ritual processes, rites of passage and group action as they lived in symbiosis with nature and the cosmos. The Aymara people of the Andes see the past as being in front of them, with their backs to the future. Standing in the present day, the path of the past is etched into the landscape with all the actions and experiences that have led us to where we are now. These tracks are our signposts, our breadcrumbs to help us find our way. By engaging with the wisdom and practices of our ancestors and early alchemists, we look towards our past in order to inform our future and establish a framework for reclaiming a sacred relationship to nature and, in doing so, ourselves. There is potential for alchemy in everything that we do, from how we respond to our experiences and navigate situations, to the ways in which we go out into nature and our community, and how we create in the personal laboratories of our homes and workplaces.

CHAPTER II

PLANT COMMUNICATION, WILDCRAFTING AND BOTANY

Plant Communication

The language of plants is a complex symphony that is holistic and holographic, expressing the whole being as one. Listening requires direct synaesthetic perception using our felt sense rather than linear, analytical processing. As we open up these channels of communication and come into a greater state of coherence, we can begin to practise listening with plants. The language of plants can be experienced in many ways, such as through the act of plant gazing, divination, floriography (the language of flowers) and direct perception. Plant neurobiologist Monica Gagliano, whose experiments include demonstrating the capacity for memory of the *Mimosa pudica* (shy plant), calls this act of deep listening with plants '*Oryngham*', which she says is plant language for 'thank you for listening'.

When we sit with a plant, information is exchanged on multiple levels. In the physical realm, plants photosynthesize to give us the energy to survive. We exchange breath through respiration and transpiration. The electromagnetic field interacts as wave-particles of light (biophotons) and sound (biophonons), and emits a toroidal field of energy – a doughnut-shaped feedback loop – that entrains with others in its environment so that we can share information with plants and each other. This quality of exchange was revered by our ancestors and alchemists, and is still revered today by many indigenous communities. Our future in the post-anthropocene is dependent on authentic dialogue with more-than-human intelligence.

In recent years, science has begun to demonstrate the complexity of the plant kingdom. Some plants, such as the Japanese canopy plant (*Paris japonica*), have 50 times more DNA than the human genome. Ferns have immense genomes and, in some species, the highest amount of chromosomes on record. Without a central nervous system or the sensory organs of a human, plants are able to see, hear, smell, taste and touch. Plants detect light using photo receptors in the membranes of cells in the plant's tip. These include phototropins, which are sensitive to blue light, so this helps them move towards the ultraviolet rays of the sun during the day. Plants see infrared light using receptors in their leaves called phytochromes. These act as a switch to turn the plant 'off' at night, and back on again when the sun comes up. Plants release a sweet-smelling hormone called ethylene that signals to their fruits when it is time to ripen. Plants can smell other plants and predators, and produce scents made up of pheromones to communicate dangers to one another or to trick potential predators. Sound recordings of caterpillars chewing leaves were found to prompt cabbages to release mustard oil as a repellent. Plants even have integrated gravity sensors, meaning they know which way is up.

Stefano Mancuso, a pioneer in the field of plant neurobiology, argues that it is our history of human arrogance and cultural prejudice that has led us to grossly underestimate plants. In his book *Brilliant Green*, he presents a sophisticated consciousness capable of recognition, memory and problem-solving. 'Plants eat without a mouth, breathe without lungs, see, taste, feel, communicate, move, despite lacking sensory organs like the ones we have,' Mancuso writes. 'So why doubt that they can think?' In many cultures and cosmologies, plants communicate in our dreams or altered states of consciousness in myriad forms, as beings, as people, as light or sound. They occupy the imaginal realms where intuition, precognition and insight lie. What future will we dream when we dream with plants?

In many ways, the plant itself is an alchemical still, with its own microsystem of distillation and transformation, transforming the rays of the sun through photosynthesis, where energy from the sunlight is absorbed into the leaves, while carbon dioxide is taken in from the air and water is taken in by the roots, producing oxygen and sugars. Through working with plants in alchemical practices and the creation of remedies, we are able to bridge the physical and non-physical worlds, taking elixirs as our guides. When we ingest a plant, we are also absorbing its planetary and environmental influences, which feeds the natural intelligence of our bodies with complex subtle information regarding adaptation and survival.

Many indigenous languages have no word for nature, as there is no concept or objectification of the natural world as outside of ourselves. It is not seen as an entity that is separate from people. Words for river and mountain are verbs – because to know nature is to be it. It is a state of *being*. In the *Three Books of Occult Philosophy* by Henry Cornelius Agrippa on elemental, celestial and intellectual magic, he describes the visceral dialogue of nature as *la langue verte*, 'the green language', considered to be a mystical divine and symbolic communication inherent in all things, and broadcasted through the airwaves by birds, whose domain in the sky is the literal intermediary between the earthly and the cosmic realms.

Those initiated in this tongue have dedicated their practice to deciphering and learning this divine language in order to converse with beings of elemental and spiritual realms. Paracelsus called this web of exchange *lumen naturale* ('the light of nature'), and mystic Hildegard von Bingen called it *viriditas* ('the greening power'). Nature is not something to be decoded with the mind alone; it is a matter of the heart and of reverence, a communion and exchange with the universe.

Go out into nature and seek a sacred space that you can return to to cultivate this language that will allow for mutual exchange of ideas and support a shared vision for the future. Keep asking yourself, how does it feel? Engaging in active imagination is the gateway to more-than-human and celestial communication. Sitting with plants that you do not have prior knowledge of can be a useful practice in developing communication, because you are not bringing assumptions or projections to the experience. Ask the plant to reveal its nature to you; you can research this afterwards. In the words of Goethe: 'The senses do not deceive, judgement deceives.'

'Speech is not of the tongue, but of the heart.'

PARACELSUS

PLANT GAZING

Sit in front of your chosen plant.
Regulate your breathing, relax your eyes and soften your gaze.
As we inhale, we receive and integrate information from the plant and the cosmic climate that it exists in, and with each exhale, we dissolve ourselves into this shared space of being.
Imagine the flow of your exhale meeting the plant, which absorbs the carbon dioxide. In return, inhale to receive the oxygen from the plant. Continue this cycle as you entrain with the plant.
When a thought or sensation arises, ask for confirmation by repeating it to the plant.
Wait for a shift – an embodied yes or no.
Give thanks to the plant for this exchange.

The more you practise plant gazing, the more you will open up pathways of communication.

BECOMING PLANT MEDITATION

Close your eyes
Breathe into your body
Drop in to the darkness that lies behind your eyelids
Here is the still point in the chaos
A refuge
And it is never not there
It is the cosmic void within
Where everything arises and passes into existence

Dissolve into this pregnant nothingness
Allowing the spaces between places within spaces
of your cells to
Expand, infuse, diffuse

Particles become waves
Fixed points of time unlock
And collapse
Into this
Prima materia
Of formlessness

From this stillness, we draw our first cosmic breath
Inhaling all potentialities
As we release with the exhale, a primordial sound
A celestial monochord

Radiates out from our formless bodies
To entangle with the stars
And we spiral through constellations
As dusty skirts of planets spin at the edge of the horizon
Like whirling dervishes
Leaving us spinning in their wake

We pass through the heart of the Sun
And Venus kisses our cheeks as
The Moon lulls and laps lunations
And we feel the gravitational pull of our planet
Calling to us

Waves become particles become waves
As packets of light and sound
We enter into Earth's atmosphere

And we are received into the leaves of a plant

We transpire, respire, transform
Held in the velvet bosom of a bloom
To pollinate and procreate and
Encapsulate
Into
A seed

And the wind hears our call
Delivering us to our destination
Nesting us into the cool, dark, damp
Soil

And we lie
And we wait
Held in the cosmic womb

And from this pregnant darkness
We begin to swell
And yearn for the touch of the Sun
Mycelium navigate our ascent
Planetary forces pull at our stalk
As we rise up

Unfurling our leaves
To meet the light that we once were
And we awaken
Becoming plant

From this space of being plant
Feel into your essence
As you embody your plant
What colours, patterns and forms appear?
Are you in flower?
Do you bear fruit?
Perhaps you feel your roots reaching into the earth
What is your texture, your aroma?
What movements want to express themselves?
Perhaps you want to move your branches or stand
tall in your trunk?
Thoughts, images, sensations might float into
your awareness
You may feel nothing and that's also information
Where does that nothingness originate from?
Can you locate it?

What is your medicine?
What is your wisdom?
What is your voice?

Clockwise from top left:
Angelica (*Angelica archangelica*),
pineappleweed (*Matricaria
discoidea*), ginkgo (*Ginkgo biloba*),
cleavers (*Galium aparine*), primrose
(*Primula vulgaris*), broadleaf plantain
(*Plantago major*), borage (*Borago
officinalis*) and wood betony
(*Betonica officinalis*).

Wildcrafting

The alchemical approach to nature and the making of remedies and elixirs is a multi-dimensional concept that begins with the opening of the senses, and makes use of meditation, intuition and knowledge of the planets and the stars to choose the appropriate timing for harvesting a plant for the preparation of a remedy. The entire cosmos is involved in this process. It is a symbiotic method of exchange, of existing in synchronicity with all that is, as the alchemist goes out into the wild with awe and wonder and *listens* to the higher intelligence at play within nature. True alchemy does not seek dominion over other beings; it is instead an act of reverence and servitude towards kin. We are being called to make *with* nature, as our guide and medium. The alchemist is an apprentice to the wild.

Wildcrafting, also known as foraging, should be a meditative process: a multi-sensory and embodied experience in communion with the land, carried out after consulting the stars and the waxing and waning of the Moon, and surveying the land for messages. Dandelion, chickweed and clover will close their petals if rain is coming; trees reveal the undersides of their leaves in the wind when a storm is brewing; sweet smells of flora are more potently carried on humid air; and dewy grass heralds a dry day. Entering into nature, we open up to receive its wisdom, paying attention to its signals and messages through patterns and signatures.

A basket is ideal for gathering plants, as it allows spores and seeds to fall through, assisting nature in its propagation. Use small cloth or paper bags for gathering seeds and for separating plants. Gloves are useful if picking nettles or plants that may cause an allergic reaction, like mugwort. Labels are useful initially, as it is easier to identify a plant whole in its habitat than when back in the lab in pieces. When gathering plants for magic and ritual, a ceremonial knife with a white handle is traditionally used. Copper is preferred over iron or steel because it is conductive and supports the natural flow of the earth energies, rather than disturbing the soil's magnetism as iron would. For safety and legality, scissors may be used. A small hand trowel or fork is used for roots. Much of harvesting is about using common sense, which is supported by being present in the moment and alert to one's surroundings.

Out of respect to nature and its abundance, make an offering in exchange for anything that you take. This can be a *verbal* prayer asking for the plant's permission to pick it or to work with it and giving gratitude, or a *physical* offering, such as a pinch of tobacco, or some sacred resin, herbs or seashells. Never take more than is required, and never from just one plant. For this reason, the remedies in this book are formulas based on ratio, where ingredients can be adjusted based on what nature offers, and no more. Above all, give back by assisting the plant in its work by saving its seeds and scattering them. Be willing to give up the harvest of a particular plant if it is in poor supply and exchange it for another that is in abundance. Take into account the life of a plant; if you remove the entire root of a plant, that is the end of its life, and removing the blossoms from a tree in spring jeopardizes fruit in the autumn, so do so sparingly. Similarly, consider the habitat as a whole. Berries and nuts are food for the birds and squirrels, while floral nectar is sustenance for the bees.

Being aware of the seasons and availability helps you to be on the lookout for certain plants, and to time when to harvest appropriately. Seasonal calendars (almanacs) are useful guides, but nature isn't a conformist, and a warm spell in winter can trick plants into growing, while a cold spell in autumn might trigger early fruiting. Pay attention to what the plants in your local area are doing and observe them through the seasonal transitions to help you be informed ahead of time. The cycles of the Moon also give guidelines on when to sow and when to harvest plants (see page 42).

We can get a sense of the personality of a plant through meditation and direct perception, where we can witness sensations and thoughts may arise through this communication, often spoken symbolically through dreams or visions. In the forest, the ability to perceive comes from the simple act of turning up and paying attention, sitting in stillness with a plant and allowing oneself to be guided by the plants.

PRECAUTIONS

Avoid the edge of pathways where dogs do their business and ensure that foraging is permitted on the land that you are on. Research the area you plan to visit and make sure it is distanced from contaminants such as industrial waste, heavy metals, pesticides and herbicides, or neighbouring plants that are toxic or poisonous. Old graveyards often hold heavy metals in the soil from lead coffins and toxic embalming materials.

POISONOUS PLANTS

Knowledge of some of the key poisonous wild plants is a vital part of wildcrafting. It takes time to establish a relationship with a plant and to truly get to know it, particularly as it may present itself in various forms through the seasons. Confusing an edible plant with an inedible or toxic one could have deadly consequences. For accurate plant identification, it is necessary to refer to a reliable botanical guidebook. Using flora keys, practising spore printing of fungi and building a herbarium are good practices to cultivate this knowledge. Pay close attention to the Latin names of the plants, as common names can differ between regions. *Never pick or consume anything unless you are absolutely certain that it has been correctly identified.*

While the bright red berries of lords-and-ladies (*Arum maculatum*) are a distinct warning, in their early growth, the leaves are similarly shaped to those of common sorrel, and they may grow close to – and be confused with – edible wild garlic. While common hogweed (*Heracleum sphondylium*) is edible, just coming into skin contact with giant hogweed (*Heracleum mantegazzianum*) can cause photosensitivity that leads to skin blistering. Monkshood (*Aconitum napellus*) can cause paraesthesia or headaches just from skin contact. The two primary poisonous families are the Solanaceae (the Deadly Nightshade family – *Atropa belladonna*, *Datura stramonium*, *Hyoscyamus niger* and *Solanum dulcamara*) and

the Apiaceae family, which includes poison hemlock (*Conium maculatum*) and hemlock water dropwort (*Oenanthe crocata*). Many common and seemingly harmless plants such as daffodil (*Narcissus pseudonarcissus*), arnica (*Arnica montana*) and buttercup (*Ranunculus acris*) are highly toxic if ingested and should only be taken externally or as vibrational essences. Highly poisonous plants are found in controlled dosages in pharmaceutical drugs such as mistletoe (*Viscum album*) and foxglove (*Digitalis purpurea*). Many hallucinogenic plants, such as caapi (*Banisteriopsis caapi*) and mandrake (*Madragora officinarum*), contain poisonous alkaloids. See page 186 for further information on the plant families used in the remedies.

With fungi, the Amanitas are a key poisonous family, but there are many more subtle variations, with not-so-subtle repercussions, as their names suggest, emphasising how fundamental proper identification is. These include death cap (*Amanita phalloides*), destroying angel (*Amanita bisporigera*), angel wings (*Pleurocybella porrigens*) and the well-known hallucinogenic fly agaric (*Amanita muscaria*).

ENDANGERED BOTANICALS

Some key botanicals in the traditional herbal *materia medica* are at threat or endangered in some regions, including slippery elm (*Ulmus rubra*), eyebright (*Euphrasia officinalis*), goldenseal (*Hydrastis canadensis*) and echinacea (*Echinacea purpurea*). While this is a continually evolving area, it is advised to keep an eye on the endangered lists published by United Plant Savers or the Fair Wild Foundation, and to always consider conservation above all else.

Botany

The plant exists in a state of alchemy, expressing itself as a cosmic vessel, distilling its essence into its leaves, reflecting the etheric plane in its petals. In *Metamorphosis of Plants*, Goethe envisioned an archetypal plant, a primeval being that encapsulated the past, present and future expressions of all plants. The shape and form of a plant is a reflection of its relationship to the cosmos, its environment and its kin. To know the anatomy of a plant is to know it intimately, as you would the form of a lover. In the cosmology of the Tikuna people of the Colombian Amazon, the first humans originated from plants, and this is reflected in how they name the parts of a plant as parts of the human body. A plant has *nachaküü* (arms), *náchinü* (buttocks), *naparà* (legs) and a *maüñe* (heart).

Though a plant is greater than the sum of its parts, an understanding of its form and function through its anatomy is a vital resource for wildcrafting and medicine-making to ensure accurate identification. The patterns, shapes and formations of plants provide a map for identification. The arrangement of petals, the shapes of leaves and the form a stem takes can indicate which family a plant belongs to. For example, almost all plants in the mint family have square stems and opposite leaves; although this is not exclusive to this family, it is a valuable indicator. The arrangement of buds on twigs and the patterns in bark can help you to identify trees in the winter.

Flora keys list key characteristics of plants, such as the shapes and arrangements of leaves and petals. With dedication, it will be possible to accurately identify your plant based on its visual form and expression.

TAXONOMY

This is the classification of biological entities into groups. It uses Latin names to ensure that there is no confusion about which plant we are considering.

Common names are generic – when we call a rose a rose, we could be referring to any of the 30,000 and more varieties that exist across the globe – and they can also be misleading. For example, evening primrose is not actually a primrose, while Douglas fir is not a fir, but a pine. Botanical names give plants a deeper profile, and the Latin also offers clues, such as the type of habitat or form of the plant. For example, *repens* means 'creeping', and *erecta* means 'upright'.

CLASSIFICATION

A two-part system (binomial nomenclature) for classifying botanicals was established by Carl Linnaeus in his 1753 book *Species Plantarum*. The first part is the genus, which is capitalised, and the second part denotes the species and is in lowercase. Botanical names are always shown in italics. The taxonomic authority gives the name of the person who first described the species, so a species identified by Linnaeus will have the taxonomic authority 'L.' (for example, *Quercus alba* L.). The plural of species is Spp. Similar genera are grouped into a family, and large families are divided into subfamilies or tribes. Plants can be classed as flowering (Angiospermae) or non-flowering (Gymnospermae). Gymnosperms are trees and shrubs, predominantly coniferales, such as yew, juniper, Douglas fir and pine. They also include equisetales, which are considered to be living fossils, such as horsetail.

HERBARIUM

Building a herbarium of wild plants marries the experience of the wild with the wisdom of scientific classification and provides a tangible way of documenting the journey through the seasons. Plants are pressed – laid out in their truest expression so as to mimic life and ensure all parts are visible – either in a traditional press or between sheets of blotting paper or newspaper weighed down by the pages of a large book. Once dry, they are placed into a herbarium book or mounted onto cartridge paper and labelled with their common and botanical names, along with the date and location of harvest, their habitat and a description. Other sensory information can be added to this, including herbal actions and supporting references in magic and folklore to create a detailed profile. The herbarium can be mounted onto cards and used as a divinatory tool. A question is asked, and a card is picked at random, with the plant offering its energetic wisdom. You may be inspired to make a remedy, or it might be medicine enough just to meditate on the plant and tune in to its vibrational frequency and healing energy.

FUNGI

Fungi are largely absent from alchemical texts, but are impossible to ignore now that we have a greater understanding of their relationship with the ecosystem. In many ways, fungi are the ultimate alchemists of the natural world, acting as elemental magicians and decomposers by transforming the 'lead' of toxic waste products and heavy metals into 'golden' nutrients and phytochemicals by feeding back biochemical information signals into the mycelium, which then generates the necessary enzyme to break down a substance.

Fungi are evolutionary pioneers, and their ability to adapt to biological threats makes them key alchemical allies. The vast majority of fungi are thought to have direct relationships to plants. Symbiotic or mycorrhizal fungi have a mutually beneficial relationship with particular plants, such as the fly agaric (*Amanita muscaria*) and the silver birch (*Betula pendula*). Saprophytic fungi live off dead organic matter. These can exist in a dormant state within a tree, and when it declines, the fungal cells are activated; birch polypore (*Piptoporus betulinus*) is an example of this. Parasitic fungi, such as the honey fungus (*Armillaria sp.*), colonize and then live at the expense of their host, although it could be argued that these little alchemists are aware of a deeper layer at work within the intelligence of nature, and are working to speed up the decay of a tree which, while appearing to be healthy on the outside, has already been programmed for a future disease. Understanding these relationships is a useful identification indicator.

The fungi that we see above ground are the fruiting bodies of much larger subterranean fungal organisms. They can produce annually, like honey fungus, or as perennials, such as bracket fungi or polypores (*Ganaderma spp.*). Key identification points are gills or spores, colour and odour, sap, texture, skirting or rings around the stem. Spore samples are matched for identification. To do this, a fresh mushroom is placed gill-side down onto a sheet of glass or paper and covered with a glass to protect it from airborne disturbances. It is then left for a few hours (possibly overnight) until a clear print remains.

CHAPTER III

THE ALCHEMY OF PLANTS, PLANETS AND PEOPLE

Sensory Botany

We observe the habitat of a plant and the quality of its environment, be it hot, cold, wet or dry. A wild plant will grow where there are the conditions to support its unique needs, and often where it can serve a purpose. An example is rosebay willowherb (*Chamaenerion angustifolium*), commonly known as fireweed or bombweed, and so named because of its ability to grow rapidly out of the ashes where other plants would struggle. As it grows, it replaces the lost nutrients in the soil and prepares the way for other plants to join it. From a pathological perspective, plants growing near water may be appropriate for treating imbalances of fluids in the body, such as in the lymphatic and urinary systems. Similarly, plants growing in harsh conditions may be able to strengthen and tonify (or give structure to) the body.

From the morphology of a plant we can observe its texture, structure, form and gesture, which gives an indication of how the compounds of a plant will interact within the body. Rubbing horse chestnut (*Aesculus hippocastanum*) seeds between your palms will create a foam that indicates the saponins (from the Latin for 'soap') within, used by the plant as a microbial barrier. These are also where soapwort (*Saponaria officinalis*) gets its name from. Saponins, such as those in chickweed (*Stellaria media*) can relieve inflamed mucous membranes and act as a demulcent and expectorant, easing congestion in the lungs. Similarly, plants like broadleaf plantain (*Plantago major*) or seaweeds containing mucilages and gums can form a gel-like binding substance that can soothe inflamed tissues in the digestive and respiratory tracts.

The doctrine of Signatures draws correspondences between the shape and form of plants and the shape and form of the organ or body part that they act upon. For example, wound herbs often have a lanceolate leaf shaped like a spear or knife, while sticky resins have a similar binding quality in the body, clearing mucus from the lungs. Orchid comes from the Latin for 'testicle', and as such is used in traditional medicine for treating impotence and sterility in men. Walnuts resemble the human brain and contain omega-3 fatty acids and polyphenols that support mood and cognitive health, while the perforated petals of the wound herb St John's wort (*Hypericum perforatum*) look like broken or irritated skin. The heart-shaped fruit of foxgloves (*Digitalis purpurea*) is a signature of the cardiac glycosides within the synthesized modern heart drug, Digoxin.

Plants are like people. When we are introduced to them, we might make certain observations or assumptions. Over time, we get to know their expressions, quirks, mannerisms and personalities, and our relationship develops. It is one thing to know its chemistry, but it is quite another to spend time with a plant in its natural environment: to sit with it, draw it, smell it and taste it.

Occult and alchemical texts place much emphasis on the above-ground morphology and habits of plants, but in order to fully know a plant, we must consider its underground forces: its roots, soil and connection to the bacteria, insects, earthworms and mycorrhizal network. The depth and strength of roots are an indication of a plant's elemental forces. For example, consider the hardy root system of comfrey (*Symphytum officinale*). Commonly known as knitbone, it is used in folk medicine to literally knit bones back together. The type of soil that a plant grows in will also indicate its nature. Juniper (*Juniperus communis*) and horsetail (*Equistem arvense*) like to grow on silica-rich chalk and clay respectively.

The mycorrhizal network (from the Greek words *mykós*, meaning 'fungus', and *riza*, meaning 'root') is made up of superfine hair-like tubes called hyphae, known collectively as mycelium. These 'fungus-roots' travel through the soil and wrap themselves around the roots of plants. After a chemical courtship, the plant chooses to 'let the right one in'. The fungi help the plant access water, and provide nutrients such as nitrogen and phosphorus that the plants lack the enzymes to extract from the soil themselves. Fungi are unable to photosynthesize, so in return for their services, plants

supply valuable sugars. This symbiotic relationship was established early on in evolution, and the partnership between algae and fungi was a precursor for the existence of land plants. The majority have direct and often (but not always) symbiotic relationships with plants and may be indicators for identification and condition; for example, birch polypore (*Piptoporus betulinus*) only grows on birch trees and turkey tail (*Trametes versicolor*) on dead and dying wood.

Mycologist Paul Stamets estimates that each footstep we take impacts 300 miles of mycelium, and we are walking on the crown of what he calls the 'neurological network of nature'. This giant woodland brain, firing messages along neurological pathways to every cell, every plant, every tree, acts as an information superhighway that connects the entire system that we are part of.

Using our full spectrum of senses, we are able to know a plant through its taste, smell and colour. The bitter glycosides of wormwood, the sweet fructose levels of an apple or the isothiocyanate heat of horseradish on the tongue are all expressions of chemical and energetic forces. By crushing an aromatic plant between our fingers and inhaling the volatile oils, we enter into an olfactory library, reading the properties within a plant which will defend it against attack, and heralding constituents that are antibiotic, antifungal and antiseptic. Smell functions in humans on physical, emotional and mental levels, such as the uplifting aroma of mint or the soporific qualities of lavender.

A plant may use colour to attract pollinators or repulse predators. These frequencies of light reflect the vibrational resonance of a plant, and give an idea of its psycho-spiritual properties, which have correspondence to systems such as the chakras and planets. Colours are also indicators of phytonutrients. For example, chlorophyll is green, and contains a central atom of magnesium, so the greener the plant, the more chlorophyll – and therefore magnesium – it contains. Flavonoids (from the Latin for 'yellow') are responsible for the bright canvases of fruits,

berries and flowers, and contain a number of properties that include antioxidant and anti-inflammatory effects. Carotenoids produce a combination of yellow, orange and red, and stain plants with anthocyanins to produce pinks, reds, magentas and blues. Anthocyanins are pH sensitive, so flower colour will vary according to soil acidity.

Plants consist first of primary metabolites, which perform vital life-giving functions, such as amino acids and proteins responsible for cell division, growth and reproduction. Similarly to humans, certain vitamins, minerals and macronutrients, like carbohydrates and fat, are necessary to fulfil basic biological functions. They also consist of secondary metabolites, such as alkaloids, phenols and terpenoids, which protect the plant from biological and evolutionary influences, such as pathogens, and are antibacterial, antifungal and antiviral. These actions are also of therapeutic value to humans. Plants also use secondary metabolites to attract the predator of the insect attacking them in an act known as mutualism. Each plant has its own package of phytonutrients, some with higher qualities of a certain mineral or vitamin. For example, nettles (*Urtica dioica*) are high in iron, horsetail (*Equisetum arvense*) in silica and rosehip (*Rosa canina*) in vitamin C.

The largest group of secondary metabolites are phenols: the aromatic antioxidant and anti-inflammatory compounds that include phenolic acids, flavonoids, tannins, stilbenes, curcuminoids, coumarins, lignans and quinones. Alkaloids (signified by the suffix 'ine') are also widespread and mostly found in flowering plants. They are usually potent in action, with examples including the atropine that dilates pupils found in deadly nightshade (*Atropa belladonna*), the antimalarial quinine in cinchona (*Cinchona officinalis*) and the many sedative pain-killing opium alkaloids found in poppy (*Papaver somniferum*), including morphine and codeine.

Taste

Taste is a primary indicator of the chemistry of plants and is related to the elemental spectrum. Herbal actions are not defined as a taste in the classical sense, but as a mouth sensation, which is why we also talk of aromatics and astringents. A plant can be both sweet and bitter, working on multiple layers. As to their correspondence to the elements, there are variations, but we can consider fire to be pungent, salty and sour; air to be astringent, bitter and pungent; water to be sweet and salty; and earth to be primarily sweet, but also sour, astringent and bitter. Other sensations include an oiliness produced by lipids and fatty acids; stickiness from resinous coatings; tingling sensations from volatile oils; and foaminess from saponins.

The salt taste is a sign of mineral content, which is nourishing to the body; it gives structure to fluids and particularly supports chronic conditions. Energetically, salty herbs provide a sense of security and support.

Bitters are wide-ranging and not confined to one chemical class, but consist primarily of terpenoids, iridoids and alkaloids. Many alkaloids are toxic, and so we see the bitter principle as an evolutionary mechanism to avoid poisoning. Taste for bitters only develops after childhood, when an individual can discern poison from cure. The bitter taste affects the digestion through a reflex action from the tongue, which stimulates the appetite by promoting gastric and glandular secretions and supporting the bile in the liver and gallbladder to aid metabolic processes. Bitters can be both cooling and heating, and stimulating and relaxing in their action, moving body heat to the digestive system, and toning the waters of the body. Bitters need to be tasted to trigger their medicinal effects. Energetically, bitter herbs help to raise vibration and lift depression. Constituents that are bitter are alkaloids (active ingredients), anthraquinones (which effect the liver), flavonoids (which are oestrogenic-like) and cyanogenic glycosides (these are sedative and antispasmodic).

Sour tastes are acids that are well represented throughout the plant kingdom, particularly in fruits.

Sour flavours are heating and stimulating, and help to shift and diffuse energy. Their presence often indicates action in the urinary tract and kidneys. Constituents that are sour are acids that reduce inflammation or swelling and protect inflamed tissue. They have an alkalizing effect and an astringent quality.

Pungent or spicy herbs are often the result of essential oils within the plant. Seventeenth-century astrologer and herbalist Nicholas Culpeper referred to the pungent taste as 'biting', which can be either hot and spicy or sharp and acrid. Its energetics are upwards and outwards, exciting the body and generally warming, stimulating, diffusing and drying. Plants create these compounds to defend themselves from pathogens, insects, parasites and infections with antimicrobial and anti-inflammatory properties that also benefit human physiology. Pungent herbs vitalize the body by dispelling cold and damp and relieve mental fog. They tend to act on the circulatory system, and constituents contain volatile oils that are antiseptic, anti-inflammatory, expectorant and carminative.

Astringents have a tightening and drying sensation in the mouth, and similar effects in the body. Astringent herbs are cooling and drying, and help to bring energies into the present moment.

The sweet taste indicates the presence of carbohydrates, fats and proteins, demulcent mucilage, inulin effects, polysaccharides (which stimulate the immune system) and saponins (which are expectorant). Plants with a sweet taste have a nourishing, building and tonifying effect on the body and usually act on the blood, glucose levels, spleen and pancreas. Carbohydrates are more or less complex chains of sugars ranging from single monosaccharides, like glucose and fructose, to complex polysaccharides, including energy-releasing starch and glycogen, cell-building cellulose and insulin, which regulates sugar in the blood. The general actions of these sweet chemical constituents are soothing, cooling, nourishing and anti-inflammatory. Energetically, they are grounding and stabilizing.

SALTY
▽ △

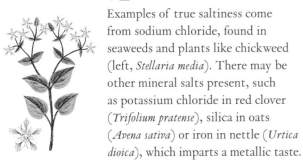

Examples of true saltiness come from sodium chloride, found in seaweeds and plants like chickweed (left, *Stellaria media*). There may be other mineral salts present, such as potassium chloride in red clover (*Trifolium pratense*), silica in oats (*Avena sativa*) or iron in nettle (*Urtica dioica*), which imparts a metallic taste.

PUNGENT
△ △

Examples are the glucosinolates of garlic and onions (*Alliums*), cabbages (*Brassicas*) and horseradish (left, *Armoracia rusticana*) that produce the isothiocyanate group of compounds. Many pungent plants exist on spice shelves, such as cumin (*Cuminum cyminum*), clove (*Syzygium aromaticum*) and cinnamon (*Cinnamomum verum*).

BITTER
△ ▽

Examples of terpenoids include aromatic monoterpenes, such as mint, sage and lavender, and antibacterial sesquiterpenes, such as dandelion (left, *Taraxacum officinale*) and wormwood (*Artemisia absinthium*), anti-inflammatory diterpenes, such as verbena (*Verbena officinalis*), and triterpenes, in wound healers, like yarrow (*Achillea millefolium*).

ASTRINGENT
▽ △

Examples include agrimony (*Agrimonia eupatoria*), oak bark (left, *Quercus robur*), walnut (*Juglans regia*) and black tea (*Camellia sinensis*), which are high in the tannins used to cure leather, and can have a similar leathering effect on the gut with excessive use, creating a barrier for nutrient absorption.

SOUR
▽ △

Examples are the malic acid in apples, ascorbic acid in rosehip (*Rosa canina*), oxalic acid in wood sorrel (*Oxalis acetosella*), and berries such as hawthorn (*Crataegus monogyna*), sea buckthorn (*Hippophae rhamnoides*) and bilberry (left, *Vaccinium myrtillus*).

SWEET
▽ ▽

Examples include polysaccharide gums and mucilages that contribute to the sweet taste, such as those in elderberry (*Sambucus nigra*), fennel (*Foeniculum vulgare*) and honeysuckle (left, *Lonicera periclymenum*). Some plants contain substances like glycyrrhizin in liquorice (*Glycyrrhiza glabra*), which create a sweet taste by stimulating receptors.

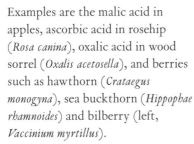

Astro-botany

We see the elements expressed through the morphology and growth patterns of plants. With the downward movement of the roots, they fix into the soil, seeking out fungal relations and nutrients in the earth element. Water mediates between the earth element and the elements of fire and air through transpiration, transporting nutrient-rich fluids through the stem to the leaves, where photosynthesis and the exchange of oxygen and carbon dioxide occurs as the air element. Water maintains the stem and provides structure to the overall plant form. The fire of the Sun allows for water and carbon dioxide to be transmuted through photosynthesis, returning the earth element as glucose, which in turn is transformed into cellulose and starch. In this way, the plant can be seen as an alchemical still with its own microsystem of distillation and transformation. The fire element is shown in the flowers and fruits as the full expression of the vital force within.

In the darkness of the soil, a seed's first action is to absorb moisture and create roots, which penetrate down into the soil in opposition to the Sun, in what is called positive geotropism (moving towards the Earth). Here we see the influence of the lunar sphere, cool, dark and moist, in the shadow of the Earth, in polarity to the hot, dry Sun. Above ground, the plant develops in the solar sphere and the stem strives forth towards the Sun in what is known as negative geotropism (moving away from the Earth). The root develops by completely turning away from the Sun's sphere, just as the Moon manifests itself most perfectly as a full moon in opposition to the Sun. The entire planetary system is reflected in the rhythm of a plant, with each part of the plant reflecting the influences and correspondences of planets, and its development interrelated to the forces of the zodiac. The planets closest to Earth influence the more mundane aspects of growth and regular functions, while the distant plants influence the more existential qualities of life and reproduction.

Mercury is the conductor of many life processes in the plant. It acts as the mediator between the *as above* sulphuric light forces of sunlight and carbon dioxide, and the *as below* physical substances of the sugars and starches and sap, giving life to the entire plant. If we compare the leaf to Mercury and its position in the solar system, the movement of both leaf and planet are influenced by the Sun, while lunar forces rise through the root as water to permeate it from within. Similarly, Mercury unites within itself the rhythms of the Sun and Moon, just as the leaf unites the gaseous carbon dioxide and sunlight with water into living substances.

The plant progresses through the planetary system as it develops, and always from a geocentric perspective, as every force of interaction is always being called back into the Earth. As it moves forward, it transcends the limitations of its basic form and expresses its individual character through its blossoming. The influence of the Moon, Sun, Mercury and Venus in the roots, stem, leaves, and perianth and pistil, which govern the fundamental life processes and create substances, weakens as the influence of the water element recedes with Mars, Jupiter and Saturn, expressed through the stamens, ovary and pollination, fruits and seeds. It is through these unique signatures that the plant determines the future expression of itself.

PLANT PART	PLANETARY INFLUENCE
THE SEED	SATURN
FRUIT	JUPITER
OVARY	MARS AND JUPITER
STAMENS	MARS
PERIANTH AND PISTIL	VENUS
LEAVES	MERCURY
CENTRAL SHOOT	SUN
ROOT	MOON

PLANETARY AND ELEMENTAL INFLUENCES ON PLANT GROWTH

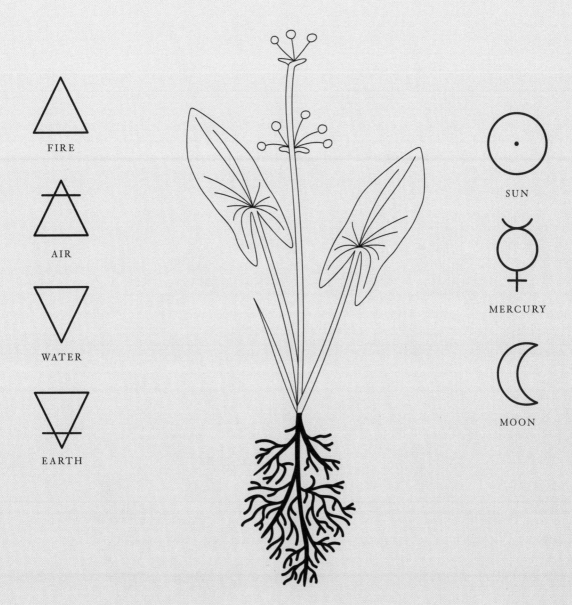

FIRE

AIR

WATER

EARTH

SUN

MERCURY

MOON

The Physic Garden

The Arabic word for alchemy – *al kīmiyā* – is thought to be derived from the Egyptian name for the fertile black silt that would appear with the annual rains, fertilizing the soil and gathering at the base of the Nile River Valley. This was how alchemy became known as the Black Art. *Al* means 'the divine', and *kīmiyā* from early Kemet, later the precursor for chemistry, so we see alchemy as divine chemistry, the spiritualization of matter. When we cultivate land, it is the nature and quality of the soil that we first engage with and transform. The creator of the biodynamic method, Rudolf Steiner, said that plants themselves could not be diseased as they were products of a healthy etheric world, but instead they are afflicted by the diseases of their environment, particularly the soil, and so we should look there for imbalances. In the biodynamic system, earth zodiac signs govern roots, water signs the leaves, air the flowers and fire the fruit and seeds.

Early evidence of the use of medicinal plants was discovered by archaeologists in a cave in Shanidar, Iraq. Pollens of medicinal plants were found lining the grave of a Neanderthal man, dating back to 60–80,000 years ago. Many plants, such as cinchona (quinine), rubber and tobacco, have changed the course of history, and modern pharmacology owes a great deal to the plant kingdom.

Many 'weeds' are medicinal plants – such as greater celandine (*Chelidonium majus*), hairy bittercress (*Cardamine hirsuta*), ground elder (*Aegopodium podagraria*) and herb Robert (*Geranium robertianium*) – and are under the Moon's reproductive and generating influence. With the biodynamic method, weeding is achieved by treating the soil so that it is resistant to these lunar forces. This is done by gathering the seeds of the weed that you want to remove, burning them to ash and scattering them on the soil. The ash represents the opposing force to the Moon.

Traditional physic (medicine) gardens were intrinsic to monasteries, hospitals, medical collages and royal courts, and were often planted by family, herbal action, body system or astrological correspondence.

Use the information and illustrative diagrams in this chapter on body systems, elements, planets and the zodiac to create a layout that most resonates with you. The plan opposite demonstrates how you might create elemental borders to grow plants with correspondences to earth, water, air and fire. The central wheel is divided into 12 segments that relate to the zodiac and body parts, and plants are chosen for their relevance (see pages 46–47 for more details on zodiacal rulerships of the body). The inner circle is divided in half for lunar and solar plants. When planning your garden, consider the different requirements for sun or shade, moisture, soil types and companion planting to create mutually beneficial plant communities. Use the information in the Alchemical Herbal to choose your plants according to their elemental or astrological correspondence.

> 'In every apple you are eating Jupiter; in every plum, Saturn.'
>
> RUDOLF STEINER

**Rosemary
(*Salvia rosmarinus*).**

PHYSIC (MEDICINE) GARDEN PLAN

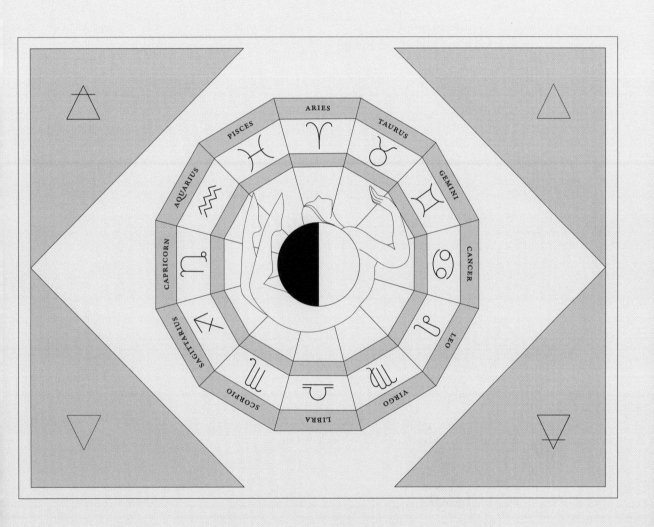

Cycles

Annuals complete their entire life cycle from seed to death within one year or one season. Biennials complete their cycle over two years, becoming dormant in the winter of their first year before another year of growth, and eventually dying. Perennials (often referred to as herbaceous perennials) have a similar process of alternating growth and dormancy, but live beyond these two years, flowering and fruiting every year that the conditions are supportive. Knowing these life cycles is important for wildcrafting and cultivation; for example, burdock root should always be harvested in the autumn of the first year, at the end of its growth, or the spring of the second year, before it sends up its shoot and, with it, its vital force and valuable nutrients. Above-ground parts are best harvested in the morning, and roots towards the end of the day.

Yarrow
(*Achillea millefolium*).

LUNAR PHASES

The influence of the luminaries of the Sun and Moon on plants are greater than all of the other planets combined. The Moon governs fertility, growth and reproductive forces, and its influence on plants and the soil varies throughout each monthly lunar cycle, providing a template for appropriate cultivation and harvest times. The time between one new moon and the next is a full lunar cycle, also called a lunation. The lunar phases are also divided into quarters (see opposite). During the first and second quarter moon phases, as the Moon waxes towards fullness and the influence of its gravitational pull increases, the active principles of the plant, sap and its vital force are drawn up to the aerial parts, making the full moon an ideal time to gather leaves, fruits and flowers. During the third and fourth final quarter phases, as the Moon and its influence wanes and the nights grow darker, the energy sinks down into the roots, making the dark or new moon the time for harvesting roots. The balsamic moon is the waning crescent or dark moon three days before the new moon, when the moon is less than 45 degrees behind the sun. Traditionally, herbs for removing disease were gathered during the waning moon, and herbs to nourish and increase vitality were picked during the waxing moon.

WAXING MOON	SOW, TRANSPLANT, BUD, GRAFT.
WANING MOON	PLOUGH, CULTIVATE, WEED, REAP.
1ST PHASE – NEW MOON TO 1ST QUARTER	PLANT ABOVE-GROUND CROPS WITH EXTERNAL SEEDS AND LEAFY, HERBACEOUS ANNUALS.
2ND PHASE – 1ST QUARTER TO FULL MOON	PLANT ABOVE-GROUND CROPS WITH INTERNAL SEEDS, FRUITING AND FLOWERING ANNUALS.
3RD PHASE – FULL MOON TO LAST QUARTER	PLANT BELOW-GROUND ROOT CROPS, BULBS, BIENNIALS, PERENNIALS.
4TH PHASE – LAST QUARTER TO NEW MOON	REST AND MAINTENANCE.

PHASES OF THE MOON FOR CULTIVATION

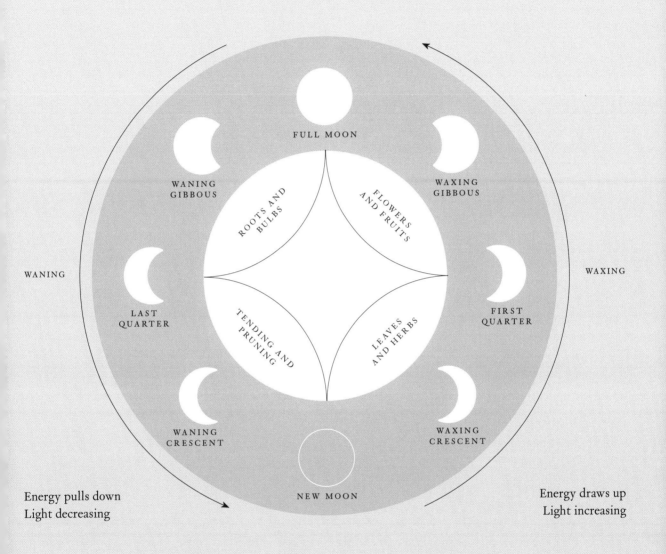

FULL MOON

WANING GIBBOUS

WAXING GIBBOUS

WANING

WAXING

LAST QUARTER

FIRST QUARTER

WANING CRESCENT

WAXING CRESCENT

NEW MOON

ROOTS AND BULBS

FLOWERS AND FRUITS

TENDING AND PRUNING

LEAVES AND HERBS

Energy pulls down
Light decreasing

Energy draws up
Light increasing

PLANETARY PHASES

Each day of the week and each hour of the day is ruled by a planetary body. Plants are gathered when the energies are high, the sap is up and the desire for the day is strong. Once picked, they should be handled with delicacy and not touch the ground again to maintain their vibrational integrity. Use this chart (right) to calculate the appropriate planetary times for harvesting and medicine making (1–12 repeats for the 24 hour cycle).

In terms of seasonality, each plant has a specific temporal matrix and a particular peak moment for each of its parts, like St John's wort (*Hypericum perforatum*), which is picked at noon on the summer solstice. In general, a good time to harvest is in the morning when the dew has lifted from the plants (although the dew itself can be gathered for alchemical purposes). Plants track the seasons by way of photoperiodism, prompting them to perform biological functions at the appropriate time.

ZODIAC PHASES

The zodiac is a system of twelve constellations that create a cosmic clock guiding the passing of time through the seasons (opposite). The signs of the zodiac can be thought of as the procession of the seasons through the sky as observed over the course of a year, associated with the orbit of Earth around the Sun.

The astrological year begins with the spring equinox, when days are equal, in the sign of Aries. Each sign emanates a particular celestial quality that reflects the energy and movement of the seasons through a physical, mental, emotional and spiritual lens, and enters the mind and body as a living energy.

PLANETARY DAYS AND HOURS

HOUR	SUN	MON	TUE	WED	THU	FRI	SAT
1	☉	☽	♂	☿	♃	♀	♄
2	♀	♄	☉	☽	♂	☿	♃
3	☿	♃	♀	♄	☉	☽	♂
4	☽	♂	☿	♃	♀	♄	☉
5	♄	☉	☽	♂	☿	♃	♀
6	♃	♀	♄	☉	☽	♂	☿
7	♂	☿	♃	♀	♄	☉	☽
8	☉	☽	♂	☿	♃	♀	♄
9	♀	♄	☉	☽	♂	☿	♃
10	☿	♃	♀	♄	☉	☽	♂
11	☽	♂	☿	♃	♀	♄	☉
12	♄	☉	☽	♂	☿	♃	♀

Planting by the zodiac supports the relationship of the elements. For example, sow lettuce during a water sign, as it emphasizes leaf growth, while a root like carrot should be planted during an earth sign. It is advised not to plant in the signs of the bowels (Virgo), head (Aries) or heart (Leo), but it is good practice to plant in the signs of the breast (Cancer) or neck (Taurus).

WHEEL OF THE YEAR

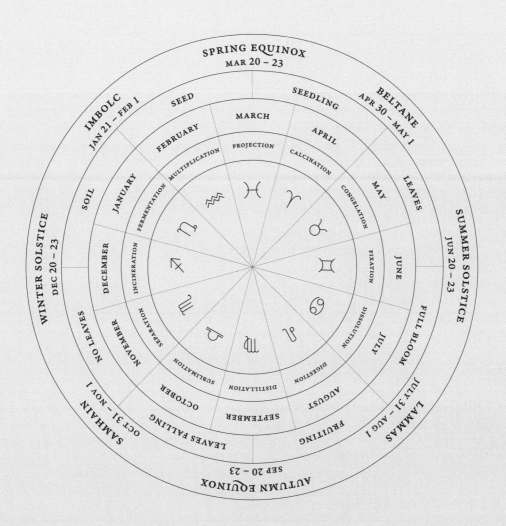

Astro-anatomy

In alchemy and astrology, we are working with archetypal forces and from the perspective of our earthbound reality. Planets are considered as all visible celestial bodies, including the luminaries of the Sun and Moon. The sacred seven inner planets include the Sun, the Moon, Mercury, Venus, Mars, Jupiter and Saturn, representing the universal harmonic matrix that frames our existence here on Earth. In esoteric and some modern astrological systems, the outer planets of Neptune and Uranus are included, along with Pluto, despite it not having astronomical planetary status. The qualities and dynamics of the planets impact all aspects of our lives, influencing not just our emotional and mental bodies but also our physiology. Each planet has a particular relationship to bodily parts and functions. For example, Mercury relates to the nervous system, and Jupiter to the liver. Equally, each zodiac sign shares a particular frequency in the body, beginning at the head with Aries and ending at the feet with Pisces. See the chart opposite for the anatomical correspondences with the zodiac signs and planets using modern rulerships. Culpeper compared the study of physick (medicine) without astrology to a lamp without oils.

Each zodiac sign is 'ruled' by a particular planet that infuses it with its energy signature. 'Rulerships' are relationships. Some planets have dual rulerships to include modern rulers based on the later discovery of planets. Each planet has a particular action on the body, and each zodiac sign rules a part of the body (see opposite).

The way in which the energies of the plants and planets are received into the body are through the elements. Our bodies are like an internal weather system of evaporation, condensation and distillation. Blood runs like the tributaries of a river through our veins and the cilia in our lungs resemble coral. The water element is all fluid secretions in the body, directly operating through the kidneys and urinary tract, as well as the lymphatic system. The earth element rules the bones, teeth and minerals as they provide the solid foundation upon which our tissues rest upon. The fire element is our vital force and heats up our body, breaks down and digests our food, and circulates the blood via the heart. Our lungs and respiratory tract bridge us to the air element, and our thinking self, electrical impulses, nervous system and our higher perception to the aether. In the inner distillation process, fire warms up and expands the cool contracted earth element in the body to burn through toxins and eliminate digestive by-products. Fire boils the waters of the body, causing them to evaporate through the air element as sweat or through the elimination channels, which are the lungs, skin, bowels, kidneys and lymph. Water can put out the fire in the body and cause damp stagnation if there is too much water or too little fire. Air mobilizes the other elements and fans the fires of the body, distributing and assisting with circulation and flow. Water mediates between the earth element and fire and air. Water moisturizes the earth element in the body, lubricating and mobilizing the vital force within. Earth gives form and structure and provides a container for water to flow while it nourishes and grounds the air element.

We also see this reflected during our inner psycho-spiritual distillation process. The fire of our inner sun, our inner wisdom and insight shines down on the parts of us that are stagnant, and onto the shaded parts of our internal landscape. This then activates and purifies, warming the waters of our emotions, which are literally released by water though the rains of our tears. Through the air element, we are able to process and influence our breath by the waxing and waning moon as we laugh and sigh.

ZODIAC SIGNS WITH PLANETARY AND
ANATOMICAL RULERSHIPS

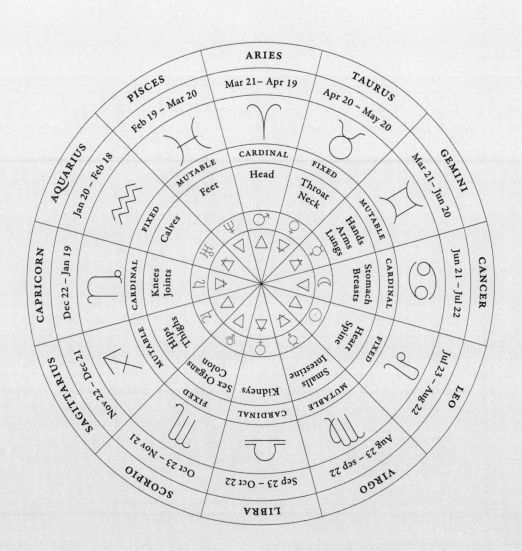

Body Systems

DIGESTIVE SYSTEM

Gastrointestinal tract, digestion, assimilation of nutrients and excretion. Salivary glands, tongue, oesophagus, stomach, liver, gallbladder, pancreas, duodenum, small and large intestines, anus and rectum. Supports pH balance and microbiome. Holds energetics of anger, jealousy, resentment and rage. All elements are present in the digestive system. *Plants: Fennel (left), marshmallow, chicory, milk thistle, yellow dock, peppermint, ginger, cinnamon, liquorice.*

CIRCULATORY SYSTEM

Cardiovascular system of arteries, capillaries, veins, heart, coronary vessels. Responsible for blood purification, tonifying the heart, supporting the liver, managing stress and tension. Influenced by intimacy and love. *Plants: Hawthorn, yarrow, rosemary (left), ginger, cayenne, motherwort, ginkgo biloba, horse chestnut.*

RESPIRATORY SYSTEM

Nose, nasal cavity, pharynx, larynx, epiglottis, thyroid, trachea, lungs. Skin forms part of this system as the major primary organ of oxygenation and elimination. Lungs hold sadness, longing and grief energetics. *Plants: Thyme (left), agrimony, mullein, elderflower, coltsfoot, lungwort, angelica, hyssop, horehound, oregano, sage, peppermint.*

REPRODUCTIVE SYSTEM

Organs of reproduction (male and female). Rules sexuality, desire and attachment. *Plants: Evening primrose, hop, lady's mantle (left), damiana, crampbark, motherwort, shepherd's purse, chaste tree.*

NERVOUS SYSTEM

Central nervous system (CNS) includes the brain and spinal cord. Peripheral nervous system (PNS) connects the CNS to the rest of the body and includes the autonomic nervous system which regulates involuntary processes (including the parasympathetic, sympathetic and enteric nervous systems) and the somatic nervous system regulates voluntary processes. *Plants: Ginkgo biloba, common lime (left), chamomile, hops, passionflower, linden, gotu kola, poppy, St John's wort.*

URINARY SYSTEM

Kidneys, bladder, renal system. Eliminates water-soluble waste, balances pH in blood, regulates blood pressure and volume, controls levels of electrolytes and metabolites. Tonifies and regulates bodily fluids, supports skin function as well as elimination, relates to the adrenal glands, influenced by stress and anxiety. *Plants: Nettle, dandelion, celery, burdock (left), borage, elder, fennel, wild carrot, uva ursi.*

LYMPHATIC SYSTEM

Immune system, pathogen detection, defence and elimination through the glandular system of lymph nodes, spleen and thymus, all acting as filtration systems. Balances water within the system, connects to emotional flow and sensitivity to environmental pressures and influences. *Plants: Birch (left), cleavers, echinacea, elder, astragalus, boneset, rosehip, reishi, shiitake.*

ENDOCRINE SYSTEM

Hormonal system of glands, inclusive of pineal, pituitary, thyroid, hypothalamus, adrenals, pancreas, ovaries, testes. Stress, anxiety, tension, adrenal exhaustion, fight or flight. The word 'hormone' comes from a Greek word that means 'to set in motion, to arouse'. *Plants: Red clover (left), nettle, bilberry, astragalus, seaweeds.*

MUSCULOSKELETAL SYSTEM

Muscular and skeletal system of bones, ligaments, joints, connective tissues, muscles. Structure, rigidity, weight of responsibility or burden. Holds tension and emotional stress. *Plants: Comfrey, chickweed, calendula (left), violet, plantain, arnica, horsetail, meadowsweet, willow.*

REMEDIAL APPROACH

A remedy may be sympathetic in nature, which means that it has a similar energetic structure to the condition, so you are essentially fighting fire with fire. On the other hand, a remedy may be antipathetic, such as using a cooling plant to reduce inflammation, like cooling fire with water. As alchemy is a multidimensional approach, this 'law of similars' is often applied as it works with the natural immune responses of the body, encouraging its own process rather than working in opposition, where there can be a risk of suppressing symptoms.

Herbalist Matthew Wood views every healing plant as the embodiment of a conflict in the environment which has to be reconciled, so the remedy (which is similar to the condition), teaches the organism how to handle it, sympathizing with its experience. We are looking for plants that have a similar resonance to both the person and the condition, because we are looking towards the root cause or fundamental conditions that created the initial grounds for the disease. A condition arising in one person may present entirely different symptoms in another. They may share the same diagnosis, but the ways in which their bodies behave, the unique qualities within the elemental spectrum and the initial grounds that saw the disease manifest may be very different.

Elemental Pathology

Aristotle documented the subtle nature of the elements through the qualities of hot, cold, dry and wet. Air is considered warm and moist, water cold and moist, earth cold and dry and fire dry and hot.

Heat is a transformational dynamic and destructive force that breaks down and disperses, changing the state of being of one thing to another. It is quick, upward and outwards in energy, and creates excitation, activity and stimulation in the body, supporting digestion, detoxification and overall vitality. In excess in the body, it can create inflammatory conditions, pain and overactive immune response. Its opposite is cold, which condenses, contracts, compresses and draws together. It is slow, downwards and inward in energy. In the body, cold is slowing, and creates stagnation, lack of circulation, sluggishness and low immunity.

Dryness creates structure, texture and boundaries, and hones the shape of a thing. It is the banks of the river that provide guidance and structure to the flow of water. In the body, excess dryness can lead to deficiencies of hydration and nutrition, and poor elimination through excessive barriers. Nothing can flow in a dry desert. Drying remedies will cause moisture to leave the body, which can be achieved through increased urination (diuresis), increased sweating (diaphoresis) and increased secretions into the digestive and respiratory tracts. Wet is the opposite of dry; it is mutable and expansive, and it flows, morphs, and lubricates the system.

The humoral system evolved with the influence of Hippocrates, though it is ultimately rooted in Egyptian and Mesopotamian systems. It is based on the four humours of yellow bile, blood, phlegm and black bile, corresponding to fire, air, water and earth respectively. Galen later expanded upon this with the four temperaments of choleric, sanguine, phlegmatic and melancholic, describing the personality types associated with these qualities, which correspond to the Jungian functions (intuition, thinking, feeling and sensation). Persian alchemist Ibn Sina, known as Avicenna, developed these as aspects of mental health, emotional health, morality and self-awareness. Together, they describe a system of balance and the interactions of the elements, and how one relates to another, and how they can be applied to herbal medicine. There is a creative and destructive cycle at play within the elemental relationship, as one gives rise to or takes away from another. The twelve qualities of the four elements are observed in the body through direct perception as: the roughness, smoothness, hardness, softness, heaviness and lightness of earth; the hot or cold nature of heat in fire, the cohesion or flow of water; and the expansion or contraction of air.

'Our tears, sweat and blood are salty, and our wounds are healed by the alchemical salt.'

JAMES HILLMAN

ELEMENTS AND QUALITIES

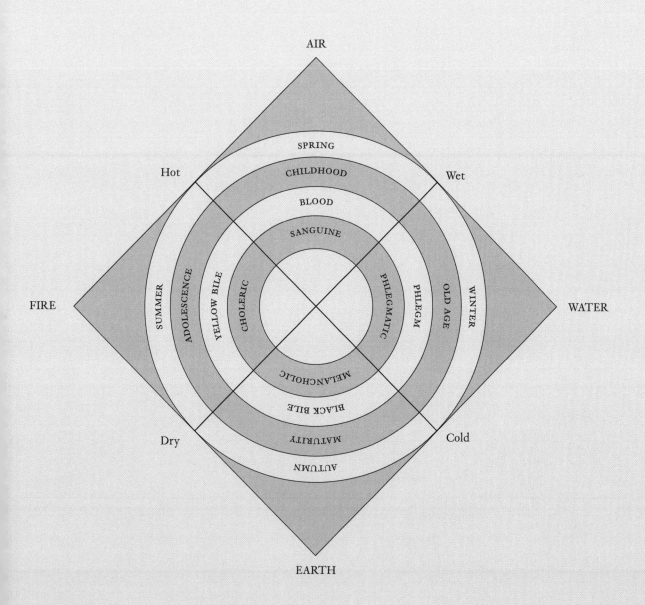

CHAPTER IV

THE ALCHEMICAL HERBAL

The Elements

The elements are qualities of matter, and form the building blocks of existence. These can be visualized as the Platonic solids named after the Greek philosopher Plato (see below). Each solid represents an element – fire, air, water, earth – which describes the ways in which energy condenses into matter as plasma, gas, liquid and solid. Aether – also 'ether' – is the spirit, the life force and consciousness that pulls the other elements together and connects the physical and non-physical realms. In alchemical preparations, the aether is known as the quintessence. Pure awareness traverses the four planes of reality through these elements as the fire of initiation and intuition, the air element of intellect and thought forms, the waters of our emotions and feelings, and the earthly sensations in physical form – the densest manifestation of consciousness. In Jungian psychology, this is reflected in the four basic functions or modes of operation of a person's psyche: intuition, thinking, feeling and sensation.

Plants do not conform to rigid structures; there are multiple correspondences, as plants are in flux and shapeshifters. They may have a tendency to express one element more than another in one moment but not the next. These systems are archetypal and fluid, so again multiple correspondences can be seen in the elements. Within these, there are resonant qualities, and those that are distorted or in shadow created in excess. There are also octaves or planes within the elements, ranging from the gross to the subtle. Western alchemists, known as 'Philosophers of Fire', positioned the transformative element of fire as central to their cosmology. These alchemists attributed four qualities or grades to fire, ranging from the gross (physical) to the subtle (spiritual). Elementary fire is the common fire of our stoves, and a separating and destructive force existing outside of the alchemist. The secret fire is the inner light of consciousness, and the life force that exists within each of us. It is the serpent or kundalini energy

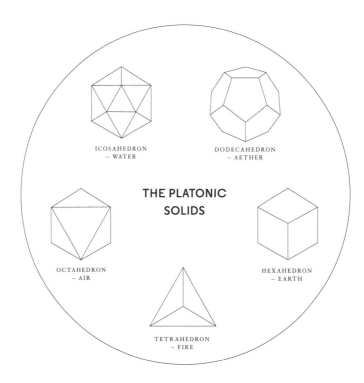

ICOSAHEDRON
– WATER

DODECAHEDRON
– AETHER

**THE PLATONIC
SOLIDS**

OCTAHEDRON
– AIR

HEXAHEDRON
– EARTH

TETRAHEDRON
– FIRE

that may lie dormant until activated and is capable of influencing and altering the physical realm, and it is coveted by alchemists as pure potential. It is a potent force that should be cultivated with caution, and for this reason, many alchemical formulas were encrypted so that only the true of heart and the initiated could access the knowledge. As theosophist H. P. Blavatsky warned, it is 'an electro-spiritual force, a creative power which, when aroused into action, can as easily destroy as it can create'. Central fire is the igniting force of creation and desire inherent in all things: an invisible animating force behind all matter, experienced through its subtle nature. Finally, the celestial fire is the most subtle form, and is the divine fire of universal consciousness.

The alchemical symbols for the elements describe the movement of the vital force. Fire is pure ascension, expressed in an upward triangle, and water is pure descension, expressed in a downward triangle. Air and earth build on these archetypal forces. Air is fire with a line across it, to symbolize that air is prone to ascension, but the moistness within limits this. Earth is water with a line across it, symbolizing a desire for descent, but that the dryness within limits the full descension of water. In alchemy, these elements are not just substances, they are energetic states. It is their dance that maintains universal harmonics and transformative processes. These elements exist on both the material and archetypal planes, and each has a dual nature and a complex symbolic web that reflects its metaphysical matrix. It is the task of an alchemist to work with these archetypal forces to transform spirit in matter and, in doing so, to enact a positive change in the material realm.

Each of the twelve signs of the zodiac is assigned to one of the four elements, originally proposed by Greek philosopher Empedocles as 'roots', and everyone is born with a particular configuration of these elements that is expressed in their physique and psyche. Elemental fire is the transformational creative force that drives our will and desires. It is the flames of our vital force, our inspiration and passion and our intuitive spirit. It is the fire in our belly and our sense of self. It governs energy production through metabolic processes. Air is our intellectual, linguistic and expressive self that inhales and exhales our experience. Air manifests as the gases in the body – carbon dioxide, nitrogen, hydrogen and methane – and the oxygen in our blood. It is responsible for the electrical currents and connections that make up our nervous system and neurology. Water is the tides within, the ebb and flow of our internal fluids and our emotional body. It guides our feeling selves, our sensitivity to our experience, our intuitive-feeling self, our memories and our subtle psychic guidance. It rules secretions and fluids, such as lymph and phlegm. Earth is our anchor to our material reality and provides structure and stability, receptivity and creation. It is the minerals in our body, and our sense of presence within a physical space and how we move within it. Aether is our connection to source, our psycho-spiritual self that desires not to be bound by ego and to be free of attachment and craving.

Earth

Classic earth constitutional types are stable, structured and have fixed, logical mentalities. The earth element is the densest aspect of our being, and physically manifests as broad and strong bone structures. Digestion and metabolism are multi-elemental processes, but ultimately reflect the systematic nature of the earth element, in particular Saturnian energies responsible for sorting, organizing and processing. Energetic imbalances can lead to a paralysis due to excess rigidity, which stifles progress and blocks intuition and inspiration, while a lack of earth causes an ungrounded, imbalanced state of detachment and confusion.

Excess earth in the body causes cooling and contraction, which can lead to an accumulation of waste products, blood stagnation, slow metabolism, fatigue, growths and abscesses, cold, and depressive physiological and chronic psychological states when a condition or trauma has gone deep through the layers of the body and become 'fixed'. Deficient earth causes malnutrition, low bone density and loss of nutrients. Excess earth is remedied by all the other elements, preferably in order of volatility, from fire to air and then water, providing movement and flow. Bitters and liver remedies help to release earth stagnation of metabolic waste in the organ. Deficient earth calls for the grounding, nourishing qualities of earth remedies, contracting and cooling bitters or astringent herbs to give tone and structure to tissues. Vulneraries act in this way to heal wounds, along with alteratives to rebuild tissue, while sweet nutritive and mucilaginous herbs will nourish, moisten and strengthen. Earth remedies often use the roots, barks and most physically dense parts of a plant to prepare powders, electuaries, poultices, cold compresses, muscle salves, balms, mineral-rich foods and infused nut oils. The earth element is particularly nourished with root vegetables, mushrooms and bone broth. Earth practices include engaging with the physical structure of the body, nature connection, reflexology, massage, yoga, movement, Qigong, forest bathing, sculpture, pottery and gardening.

Plants with a strong earth element resonance tend to be large in stature and structure, with a large surface area of influence, often deep-rooted or ground-dwelling. Earth plants are hardy, woody and dense, with solid structures, broad leaves and thick stems, such as trees and shrubs, and plants with pronounced roots and barks. Energy flows downwards. There may be brown or dark red colouring, as this colour is the slowest wavelength in the colour spectrum and corresponds to the root centre. Earth plants are ruled by Saturn and Pluto and associated with the earth signs.

The strong roots of comfrey (*Symphytum officinale*) are a signature of its grounding nature and healing potential for the structural components of the body. Primrose (*Primula vulgaris*) grows close to the ground and is one of the first flowers of spring as the earth wakes from hibernation, signifying new beginnings. Fungi express the grounding, expansive nature of the earth element through the mycorrhizal network, which transmutes the fixed above-ground body of a tree or plant into a fluid, mutable and interrelated system below.

Other plants with earth resonance include alfalfa, blackberry, black cohosh, chaparral, cypress, Douglas fir, guelder rose, horse chestnut, horsetail, magnolia, mandrake, mullein, oak, pine, plantain, sage, self-heal, Solomon's seal, vervain, walnut and yellow dock.

The psycho-spiritual energetics of imbalanced earth include fear, depression, exhaustion or overwhelm from burden of responsibility; rock rose (*Helianthemum nummularium*), mustard (*Sinapis arvensis*), olive (*Olea Europaea*) and elm (*Ulmus procera*) respectively are flower essence remedies for the extremes of these states.

Skin and
Bones Balm

Comfrey (*Symphytum officinale*) is a powerful wound-healer, and its common name, knitbone, is an indicator of its traditional use to mend broken bones. It contains the active constituents allantoin, rosmarinic acid and mucilage, which are anti-inflammatory and pain-relieving.

Comfrey accelerates the healing of sprains, fractures, torn ligaments and minor cuts, grazes and scar tissue. Despite its history as a cough remedy, it is now recommended only for external use on account of the liver-damaging pyrrolizidine alkaloids found in it. Energetically, it is grounding and stabilizing, and can help address deep-seated wounds and heal old trauma layers.

Daisy (*Bellis perennis*) is a key wound herb for bruises and skin ailments, and is a valuable alternative to arnica. It is dedicated to Ostara, goddess of spring and beauty, and Freya, goddess of love and fertility. Energetically, it encourages playfulness and purity. *Bellis* is thought to refer to the myth of a tree nymph named Belides, who turned herself into a daisy to evade an amorous pursuer. The flowers are also thought to have sprung from the tears of Mary Magdalene. The four colours of the flower are associated with different meanings: green is hope, white is faith, red is love and gold is wisdom. In folklore, a daisy chain worn by a child was believed to protect them from being stolen by fairies, while if worn by an adult, it was said it would bring them love. In the language of flowers, daisies are a symbol of innocence and virtue. Also called *flos amoris* – the love flower – the daisy asks the question 'Do you love me?'

METHOD

1 Harvest daisies and comfrey leaves when the moon is in an earth sign, and allow them to completely dry to remove any extra moisture.

2 On the next new moon, chop up the plants and pack them into a coloured glass jar, half-filling the jar and then topping up with olive oil, making sure that the oil covers the plants by a good couple of inches.

3 Cover with a muslin cloth held in place with an elastic band, and set aside in a warm place. Check regularly to ensure that the plants are well covered, agitating them a little.

4 When the moon is full, strain and weigh the oil, then use this measurement to calculate how much beeswax you will need: the ratio for oil to wax should be 4:1.

5 Gently heat the oil and wax in a double boiler or bain-marie (an invention of the alchemist Marie the Prophetess) until combined, then pour into glass pots and allow to completely set before sealing.

APPLICATION

Apply to bruises, sore muscles and minor skin ailments. Do not use on broken skin or attempt to heal broken bones that have not been set properly.

Caution: For external use only.

Water

Water types are open, expressive, sensitive and empathic, with a profound capacity for feeling. This intensity can go to extremes, reflected in the violent crashing and swelling of waves in a storm, or in the mirror-like stillness of a mountain lake. Imbalances of the water psychology can cause this energy to leak, pouring out of a person's psyche, creating weak emotional boundaries, confusion and altered states. If emotions are suppressed, this allows for the inner waters to putrefy and stagnate, and it is necessary for the inner furnace to be heated, so that through fire, the emotions rise like steam to the heart-mind to be released through tears, to transform and distil the experience. Physiologically, the water element flows through all fluids of the body, primarily through our lymphatic, endocrine, reproductive and urinary systems. The water element creates movement and flow, hydrating and lubricating the body. Deficient water restricts the flow of fluids, which can cause a build-up and retention of water, leading to an accumulation of toxins. Excess water condenses, contracts and moves down into the earth element, causing stagnation. Excess water needs fire remedies that warm and stimulate, such as astringents and circulatory tonics. Deficient water calls for water remedies that are moisturizing, such as demulcent herbs and oily nervines. Water remedies also include blood and lymph tonics, diuretics, diaphoretics, kidney tonics, reproductive tonics and sedatives. Water therapies include water-based infusions, teas, decoctions, herbal baths, body brushing, liquid extracts, hydrosols, liniments, flower essences, collecting the morning dew of plants, herbal and seaweed baths, swimming, and creating with wild botanical inks and dyes.

Water plants often have milky sap, juices or mucilages, and succulent, rounded leaves and heavy fluid storage. They tend to grow near water or in damp environments. In the body, they have downward motions, calming the nerves and pulling toxins down and out to be eliminated. They are primarily diuretic, demulcent, anti-inflammatory, emollient and expectorant, and working as a lymphagogue. Water plants are ruled chiefly by the Moon, Venus and Neptune, and are associated with the water signs.

Cleavers (*Galium aparine*) has long been a folkloric remedy for lymphatic cleansing, and it was said that drinking a cold infusion of it every day for 40 days would make you so beautiful that no one could refuse to marry you. There is some truth in this, as when the lymphatic system is clear of toxins, the skin will glow with radiance. Cleavers cools inflammation and dissolves toxic debris, pulling them and excess fluid through the lymphatic system to the kidneys, acting as a diuretic to assist in removal. With its high mucilage content, marshmallow (*Althaea officinalis*) is a very effective demulcent, soothing and cooling internal inflammation, particularly in digestive and respiratory systems, and externally cooling skin burns and rashes. Burdock (*Arctium lappa*) is physiologically cooling, alterative and a diuretic, purifying the blood and shifting stagnation and clarifying internal fluids through support of the eliminatory channels. All species of rose (*Rosa spp.*) nourish the inner waters of the heart by encouraging forgiveness, compassion and resilience in the emotional body.

Other water plants include apple, balm of Gilead, birch, bladderwrack, buckthorn, calamus, chickweed, coltsfoot, common mallow, cucumber, feverfew, hibiscus, Irish moss, jasmine, lady's mantle, lemon balm, liquorice, lovage, mugwort, myrrh, pansy, pineappleweed, poppy, red clover, rose, sea lettuce, sea purslane, self-heal, skullcap, spearmint, tansy, uva ursi, wild rose, wild violet and willow.

Psycho-spiritual complaints of water imbalances include emotional and psychic sensitivity, attachment anxiety and poor boundaries that are open to abuse; these can be remedied by pink yarrow (*Achillea millefolium*), chicory (*Cichorium intybus*) and centaury (*Centaurium umbellatum*) respectively.

Mallow Cold Infusion and Herbal Bath

Common mallow (*Malva sylvestris*, opposite), like its sister marshmallow (*Althaea officinalis*), is a highly mucilaginous and cooling plant that moistens and lubricates. It supports deficient water and dry states, such as inflammation of the mucous membranes in the digestive, respiratory and urinary tracts.

It is a key ally for excess digestive fire and coughs. *Malva* comes from the Greek word *malaxos*, meaning 'slimy', or 'to soften', while *altharea* means 'to cure'. Pythagoras recommended it for 'moderating the passions and clearing the stomach and mind', while John Gerard urged a marshmallow bath to 'take away any manner of pain'. Externally, mallow soothes, nourishes and moisturizes irritated skin. Energetically protective, it reveals power struggles and liberates the self. In the language of flowers, it means to be 'consumed by love'.

Silver birch (*Betula pendula*) is usually the first sap to flow, heralding spring and symbolizing rebirth, nourishment and protection. Its waters are deeply cleansing as a diuretic anti-inflammatory, removing excess earth built up during the winter months. Consider replacing water with birch sap in this remedy. Birch sap may be tapped by cutting a branch and draining into a bottle. Look for a tree weeping sap or put your ear to the trunk to hear it flow.

METHOD FOR INFUSION

1 When the moon is waning, gather young fresh mallow and flowers. You may include the root if this is appropriate to your needs, but never harvest a root without good reason. If including root, grate a thumb-sized piece of the root.
2 Clean, chop and place all of the plant material into a jar and fill with water.
3 Soak in the fridge overnight.
4 In the morning, strain and drink.

APPLICATION

Drink when you need to soothe and moisten inflamed mucous membranes from a cough or digestive complaint.

METHOD FOR BATH

When we soak in a bath, we are not only absorbing the water through our skin, but also entraining our inner waters with the vibration of the water. Adding plants directly to a bath – in this case, by adding the cold infusion, along with fresh leaves and petals – is a potent way of receiving their wisdom and properties. Doing this in line with the phases of the moon can help you to align with the natural cycles of emotional growth and decay. For example, a full moon is a good time to release blocked emotional charge. A new moon is a time for calling in new energies. Add flower essences and essential oils to complete the ritual.

APPLICATION

Take this bath with the cycles of the moon, or when you need emotional support.

Air

Air constitutional types tend towards a quick, alert, highly perceptive disposition, receiving and analysing information coming through on the airwaves, and poised to bolt at any minute. The challenge is to anchor these thought forms into physical reality. From an esoteric perspective, this means channelling our higher aspects into this realm, and guiding the mind into a heart space. Air-dominant physiques tend to be tall, thin and angular, and their skin cool and dry, often sensitive to the cold and subject to dry conditions. A balanced air element is hydrated through the waters of the body, and nerves and joints are lubricated with nutritional oils. An imbalance of air in the system can lead to a psychologically manic or hyperactive state and nervous exhaustion, or a feeling of being spaced out and detached, with poor memory recall. Digestive issues, muscle spasms or cramps, headaches, insomnia, dry skin conditions and lung weakness such as asthma are all possible conditions as a result of imbalance. Wind tension in the body causes a contractional response, such as when nervous tension causes the muscles to contract, or dry atrophy due to nutrient deficiency, leading to toxicity and poor elimination. Air fans the fires in the body, without which, water and earth accumulate, causing stagnation and depression. Excess air can be grounded into the earth element through nourishing roots and berries, or moistened through water remedies that are demulcent and lubricate the system. Deficient air calls for air and fire remedies, such as circulatory, brain and lung tonics. Air remedies address airborne disease, modulate cramping, spasms and electrical impulses of the nervous system, and clear excess mucous from the respiratory system through decongestants and expectorants. Air practices include burning dried herbs on coal, using diffusers, aromatherapy and essential oil blends, cleansing and purification rituals, breathwork, meditation, fresh air (time outdoors), art, movement and music therapies.

Plants that express the air element are often tall, thin, spindly and delicate, with hollow stalks with an upwards expression of vital force. Leaves are perforated, feathery and spacious, with seemingly random growth patterns. Flowers may be purple, blue or indigo in colour, which relate to the more subtle or etheric energies in terms of the chakra system. They are often high in volatile oils, making them aromatic, like thyme (*Thymus vulgaris*), meadowsweet (*Filipendula ulmaria*) and honeysuckle (*Lonicera periclymenum*). Air plant actions may be nervine, circulatory, carminative and antispasmodic. Air plants are primarily ruled by Mercury and Jupiter, and also Uranus, and are associated with the air signs.

Fennel (*Foeniculum vulgare*) is a digestive and antispasmodic plant that relieves cramping caused by excess gas and dispels mental congestion. Ginkgo (*Ginkgo biloba*), also known as the maidenhair tree, is primarily used to enhance cognition in the prevention of Alzheimer's and dementia. Common lime or linden (*Tilia × europea*) and lavender (*Lavandula angustifolia*) relax the nervous system, calming the mind and reducing anxiety. Wood betony (*Betonica officinalis*) was once considered a cure-all for everything from hangovers to snake bites and madness. It is a good air ally for alleviating nightmares, headaches and anxiety. It stimulates circulation and in doing so supports memory.

Other plants with air affiliations include agrimony, anise, bergamot, borage, broom, caraway, cardamom, catnip, chicory, dandelion, elderflower, eucalyptus, eyebright, honeysuckle, hops, horehound, lemon balm, lemon verbena, marjoram, mastic, mistletoe, mugwort, mullein, nutmeg, passionflower, pennyroyal, peppermint, pine, red clover, slippery elm, spikenard, valerian, vervain, wormwood and yarrow.

Psycho-spiritual complaints of air imbalance include mental anxiety, uncertainty and aloofness, which can be supported with flower essences of white chestnut (*Aesculus hippocastanum*), scleranthus (*Scleranthus annuus*) and clematis (*Clematis vitalba*) respectively.

Spiritus Vitae

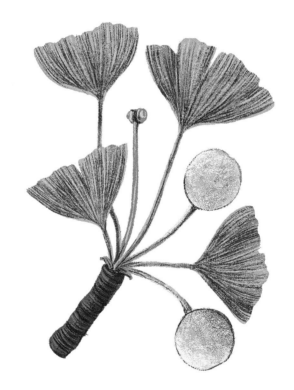

Meaning 'spirit of life', this tonic is a variation on aqua vitae, the 'water of life', traditionally made with the spirit of wine – wine that has been purified through distillation – and a combination of aromatic herbs and spices. These recipes were often highly secretive, but all were concocted with the intention of lifting the spirits, strengthening the nerves and fortifying the body against disease. Ginkgo (*Ginkgo biloba*) is the key plant here, which energetically opens clear channels for insight and ideas, clarity of thought and expression.

Ginkgo is considered to be a living fossil, as the sole living member of the *Ginkgoales*, which date back over 200 million years. Consequently, it represents longevity, strength and protection. This is reflected in its resistance to pests. High in antioxidants, it is a circulatory tonic which increases oxygen absorption in blood cells, oxygenating the brain and supporting cognitive function and memory recall. Agrimony (*Agrimonia eupatoria*) aids in the release of nervous tension, particularly in the digestive system. Energetically, it releases and protects, helping to transform intense mental energy into a healthy expression that can be vocalised. As an essence, it is a key remedy for those who put on a brave face and soldier on, despite the pain they carry inside. In the language of flowers, it symbolizes gratitude.

METHOD

1 Combine dried and chopped ginkgo leaves along with other air plants, such as fennel (seed), caraway (seed), dandelion (root), marjoram, agrimony, common lime, wood betony, mullein and wormwood, and grind them with a pestle and mortar.
2 Cover well with spirit of wine, or use homemade or biodynamic wine.
3 Take either the short or long path. The short path is allowing the plants to infuse in the wine in a bottle kept in a dark place for a full lunar cycle. Depending on the combination you use, this may require a philosophical month of 40 days. The more delicate and aromatic plants, such as ginkgo and fennel, will infuse quickly, while roots will take longer. The long path is to make a spagyric by placing the wine and plants in a cucurbit and distil seven times (see pages 100 and 178).

APPLICATION

Take a few drops as a daily treatment or 1 teaspoon when you need a pick-me-up. *Caution*: Use ginkgo in moderation, as it contains ginkgotoxin, which can be toxic in high doses. Its fruits and seeds also contain toxic compounds that are not destroyed by heat.

Fire

People with predominantly fire constitutions are energetic and wilful characters with a strong sense of passion and purpose. Physically, they are of a medium, muscular build, sometimes with a visual expression of the colour red in their hair or a flushed face, and with warm and oily skin. They have a strong digestive fire, immune defence and vital force. Excess fire in the mental-emotional body manifests as rage, irrational and reactive behaviour and insomnia, while deficient fire shows up as a lack of motivation and low self-esteem. Excess heat in the body can lead to coronary disease and chronic inflammatory disorders, causing pain and swelling. Digestive issues are created when the digestive flame is weak, limiting the ability for the body to break down and assimilate nutrients or expel toxins. If the digestive fire is too forceful, it can burn through nutrients without absorption and create acid reflux. If fire is too strong in the body, the internal waters boil and evaporate. Water is then sweated out, leading to dehydration and inflammation (from the Latin *inflammare*, meaning 'to set on fire'). Excess fire can be remedied with the water element and cool, moistening herbs, and foods, refrigerative herbs, febrifuge, rubefacient and sedative herbs, and circulatory and liver tonics. If there is not enough fire, then water is unable to flow and causes damp stagnation, slowing down the blood and lymph, causing fatigue and weight gain. Deficient fire calls for fire remedies that are warming and stimulating, such as carminatives, digestives, and blood-building and immune-strengthening tonics. Earth and air remedies will also nourish and encourage movement. Fire treatments include sweating therapies, such as sweat lodges, steam rooms and saunas, burning herbs, nettle-sting therapy, dry skin brushing, herbal candles, fire ceremonies, exercise, martial arts, theatre and dance.

Plants express the fire element through oil production, spikes and thorns, stings and serrated edges to leaves. They are usually medium-bodied, often displaying colours of reds, yellows and oranges. They taste pungent, sour and salty, with an upwards and outwards energy. Their herbal actions are often diaphoretic, cardiotonic, adaptogenic and nervine, but overall heating and stimulating. Fire plants are predominantly ruled by the fire signs.

Cayenne (*Capsicum annuum*) is a full-spectrum stimulant, regulating the circulatory system and encouraging digestive fire. It relieves pain by interrupting neurotransmitters and nerve fibres. Horseradish (*Armoracia rusticana*) and ginger (*Zingiber officinale*) are also warming herbs with analgesic potential that stimulate the vital force of the immune system and stoke the embers of digestive fire. Ginger is an overall circulatory tonic and anti-inflammatory herb; it can redirect sensations of chaos or disorder, which is reflected in the way that it alleviates nausea. Rosebay willowherb (*Chamaenerion angustifolium*), or fireweed, has anti-inflammatory properties that remedy excess fire in the body. Energetically, it opens us up for new beginnings following shock, trauma or burnout. Oily herbs, such as rosemary, and resins, such as frankincense, are traditionally used to cleanse and protect, supporting the fire element's ability to purify.

Other plants with correspondences to the fire element include allspice, angelica, arnica, basil, bay, bilberry, blessed thistle, borage, calendula, cedar, celandine, centaury, cinquefoil, clove, coriander, cumin, dill, dragon's blood, garlic, gorse, hawthorn, heliotrope, holly, hyssop, juniper, lovage, motherwort, mullein, oak, pepper, rosemary, rowan, saffron, sea buckthorn, stinging nettle, St John's wort, sunflower, thistle, walnut, witch hazel, wood avens, woodruff and yarrow.

Psycho-spiritual complaints of fire imbalance include restlessness and frustration, which can be remedied with impatiens (*Impatiens glandulifera*) essence, and rage, jealousy and hatred towards others, which can be remedied by holly (*Ilex aquifolium*).

Fire Cider

Fire cider is a warming and stimulating remedy that stokes digestive fire and boosts the circulatory and immune systems. It can help combat the winter months when the fire in our environment wanes with the reduction of the Sun, and we see an increase in cold, damp states and stagnation within our bodies. Horseradish (*Armoracia rusticana*) is a key plant in this remedy. A cure-all in the Middle Ages, it was taken as a painkiller to alleviate colds and cramps.

This remedy was made popular in the 1970s by herbalist Rosemary Gladstar, although variations of it have been in circulation amongst communities across the globe for eons. In Greek mythology, the Oracle of Delphi is said to have told Apollo that the horseradish is worth its weight in gold. Similarly to ginger (*Zingiber officinale*) and turmeric (*Curcuma longa*), it is a warming digestive and circulatory stimulant that acts as a decongestant and expectorant, clearing sinuses and excess mucus. Chilli (*Capsicum annuum*) is high in capsaicin, and also supports these functions. Onions (*Allium cepa*) are high in flavonoids and are antimicrobial, antiviral and anti-inflammatory, as is garlic, which is antibacterial and antimicrobial. Cloves (*Syzygium aromaticum*) are warming and stimulating, and contain eugenol, which is effective against harmful bacteria and fungus, and is a potent anti-viral and blood purifier. Angelica (*Angelica archangelica*) is a fire ally for the circulatory and digestive systems, and encourages reconnection and trust in the universe. The citric acid of lemons helps detoxification and mineral absorption, along with the immune support of vitamin C.

METHOD

1 Combine 2 parts sliced onion and half a part each of horseradish root, angelica root, ginger and turmeric (reduce to a quarter each for a milder flavour), with 1 teaspoon each of black peppercorns, cloves, wild thyme, rosemary and marjoram. Add 1 lemon cut into wedges, 1 cinnamon stick and 1 hot chilli pepper (remove the seeds).

2 Add a handful of berries, such as elder berries or sea buckthorn, for added immunity to the aromatic herbs already used, which have antibacterial properties.

3 Place everything in a glass jar and pour over enough raw apple cider vinegar to cover it all by a couple of inches. Add raw honey to taste and seal the jar. Allow it to develop for a few weeks before straining. You may wish to begin when the Sun moves into one zodiac sign and strain when it moves into the next.

4 You may blend the remaining plant matter and repeat the process with more vinegar for a second extraction.

APPLICATION

Take 1 teaspoon a day for fortitude and maintenance during the winter months, poor circulation or sluggish digestive fire, or at the first sign of feeling run-down. It can be diluted with warm water or soda for a tonic. *Caution*: Avoid using if you are experiencing acid-reflux or indigestion.

Aether

Aether people are psychic, open, receptive and visionary. They can also struggle to remain grounded in their bodies, and if the path of spiritual transformation is not grounded into this physical reality, psychosis can result when a person is no longer able to differentiate between this world and the extrasensory communication of an altered state. This can result in a fracturing of their psyche and parts of their own personality being reflected back to them as an external presence. It is important to assist altered states through purification and non-toxic environments. Earth remedies and grounding practices are important allies in this process. Our journey towards this enlightened state is through practices of meditation, shamanic journeying, astral projection and multi-dimensional healing modalities. Aether plants are associated with the outer planets, asteroids, and stars and systems such as Pleiades, Sirius and Arcturus.

Aether plants act as bridges to other planes of reality and may communicate in dreams, altered states, song and sacred geometries. Aether herbs play a role in clairvoyance, such as the Oracle at Delphi and during degrees of initiation into the Mysteries. They have an influence on the third eye and crown chakras, and the pineal gland. Some of these power plants are strong allies and entheogens, such as caapi (*Banisteriopsis caapi*) – the sacred vine from which ayahuasca is made – and jimsonweed (*Datura stramonium*). Indigenous groups such as the Makushi describe power plant charms – *bina* – that are seen as shamans in their own right, with the ability to cure or kill at will through energetic entities such as magic darts and the art of assault sorcery. Historically, many plants have been employed as spiritual allies. To raise the vibrations of a space in order to allow for communication with higher beings, myrrh (*Commiphora myrrha Nees*), copal (*Hymenaea verrucosa*) and frankincense (*Boswellia carterii*) resins are burnt, as is cedar (*Cedrus libani*) and palo santo wood (*Bursera graveolens*), or dried sage (*Salvia officinalis*), sweetgrass (*Hierochloe odorata*) and mugwort (*Artemisia vulgaris*). The druids used vervain (*Verbena officinalis*) in this way

for ritual cleansing, divination and the consecration of sacred space, and it was one of their four sacred herbs. Blue lotus (*Nymphaea caerulea*) wine was a ritual drink in Egypt used to access altered states of consciousness; similarly, saffron is used during fasting to align with higher states of consciousness. In Central and South America, cacao (*Theobroma cacao*) is a sacred tree, the beans of which are where chocolate is derived from. When made into a ceremonial drink, it energetically opens up the heart and purges the body through tears. In India, gotu kola (*Centella asiatica*) is called Brahmi because of its use by yogis in meditation, and holy basil (*Ocimum tenuiflorum*) or tulsi (*Ocimum tenuiflorum*) is another sacred herb used to support the spiritual path. Other psychoactive substances include mescaline from peyote and San Pedro cacti, psilocybin from magic mushrooms, cannabis from the cannabis plant and opium from the poppy.

Note that some psychoactive plants are illegal in certain countries, and are often toxic. Many are central to indigenous belief systems and sacred ceremonies, and so should not be approached without the guidance and permission of cultural and spiritual representatives. A period of purification and cleansing is often required, before working with the plant.

Other aether plants for connecting to the sacred and the liminal include African dream root, bobinsana, butterfly pea, damiana, Mexican dream herb, passionflower, rue, sun opener, valerian and wild asparagus root.

The psycho-spiritual energetics of aether imbalance include daydreaming and detachment from reality, or isolation and aloofness, which are remedied with clematis (*Clematis vitalba*) and water violet (*Hottonia palustris*) respectively.

Mugwort Smokestick

Mugwort (*Artemisia vulgaris*) corresponds strongly to the Moon and dreaming, and is a female tonic that regulates menstrual cycles. It is named after the Greek lunar goddess Artemis, the huntress who guarded the forest, women and childbirth.

Mugwort is a warming nervine herb and mood-enhancer that encourages flow, moves and guides energy around the body, and facilitates travel to otherworldly realms, lucid dreaming, psychic guidance and intuition. It is used as a lucid dream and sleep aid, and for divination and accessing altered states of consciousness. Use this smokestick before bed or sleep with the bundle under your pillow to heighten lucidity in dreams. Mugwort was used to flavour beer and is associated with comforting weary travellers. Energetically, it is a powerful protector and cleanser of psychic channels. In the language of flowers, mugwort symbolizes joy and good fortune. Highly protective, it is used to deter all manner of spells, magic and ill-will, as reflected in its folk use for dispelling worms and parasites.

METHOD

1 Gather mugwort and yarrow on Venus's day (Friday), close to a full moon. There is also the option to add other sacred wild plants, such as vervain, meadowsweet, birch, pine, yarrow, heather, juniper, rosemary, lavender and thyme.
2 Bundle your stems together and cut to an even length. Wrap the herbs tightly with twine or string, making sure the bundle is compact and nothing is loose. Make sure you have enough string left to hang it up to dry in a space where there is a good source of warm, ventilated air, and no damp.
3 Leave to dry completely.

APPLICATION

Once dry, burn the bundle to cleanse the energy of your home and create a sacred space. Always be sure to leave a door or window open when you do so, to allow the energy to flow. Light the tip of the smokestick, then blow out the flame. Waft the smoke around the room with the intention of cleansing the space of unwanted energies or lower vibrational states, and to create a sacred space for dreaming and divination if this is your intention.
Caution: Pregnant women should avoid mugwort, even in this form, as it may cause uterine contractions.

The Planets

The celestial bodies inhabiting our solar system each have a unique rhythm to their orbits, which draw geometric patterns in their cosmic wake. Each of these motions and electromagnetic frequencies form a harmonic range that was referred to by Pythagoras as *musica universalis* – the music of the celestial spheres. The subtle qualities of these radiate through the cosmos and directly influence our own subtle energetics and the *musica humana* – the internal orchestra of the human body. This planetary dance can be measured as a mathematical symphony of ratios, and as proportional from one planet to the next. A planet cannot be understood without the Sun and the other planets, since the rhythms of the other planets affect its own rhythm.

Symbolically, each planet is represented by a glyph that illustrates its energetic signature expressed through the lens of the three essentials (see below): the circle as sulphur, the crescent or half-circle as Mercury, and the cross as salt, the body, and the intersection of all elements in physical matter. The astrological glyph for Mercury is all three combined. Here, we see again the dance of spirit and soul as the astrological archetypes place the solar disc with the energies of the spirit and the crescent with those of the soul. The Earth is a circle with the cross of matter contained within it, representing the spiritualization of matter.

The three distant planets, Neptune, Pluto and Uranus – discovered in relatively recent times, and so falling outside of traditional alchemy and astrology, but used in esoteric and modern systems – are invisible to the naked eye, and are considered to be higher octaves on this musical scale of the seven visible planets. Again, we see the threefold pattern emerge within our systems and correspondences: the alchemical three essentials, the holy trinity and the three modes of astrology. With each astronomical discovery comes an initiation, transmitted into our collective consciousness, which expands our awareness to allow us to see with a new lens of perception. Neptune expands to a higher octave of the goddess Venus, emanating the vibration of the waters of the celestial heart and unconditional cosmic love. Pluto elevates the egoic will of the warrior Mars to become the higher octave as the destroyer of that which is no longer serving our evolutionary path, to align us with our sovereign power and truth. Uranus is the higher octave of Mercury, sharing qualities of electricity, flux and the visionary mind. The orbits of the outer planets are extremely slow in comparison to the inner planets, so their influences are transpersonal – cultural, generational and universal. Integrating the outer and inner planets activates our higher consciousness beyond the personal.

Each zodiac sign has an *exoteric* planetary ruler, which is the traditional or mundane material manifestation. As alchemists, we are also interested in the *esoteric* ruler, which operates on a spiritual or soul level. For example, Aries is ruled by Mars, the god of war, representing action and force of will, whereas the esoteric ruler is Mercury, the winged messenger, mediator and communicator, representing how this energy can be channelled into the mental realm, and initiating ideas and solution-based thinking. The opposite of rulership is 'fall'. Planets are either *exalted* in a sign, where they are comfortable and their influence is strengthened, or in *detriment*, where they are awkward and their influence is weakened.

THE THREE ESSENTIALS

THE MUSIC OF THE SPHERES

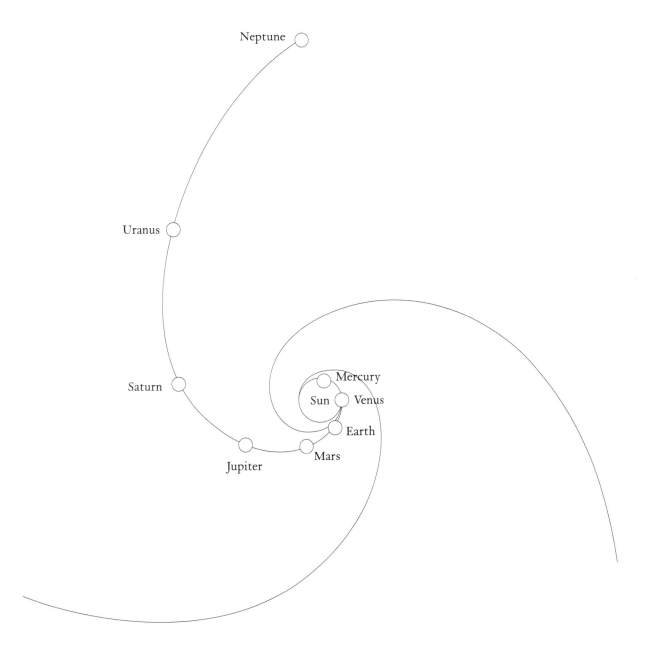

Sun

The Sun is a pure expression of the creative source, and the great central force at the heart of our solar system as its furnace lights the crucible of our existence. Its glyph is a solar disc that represents the light of the Sun as the light within our hearts, expressed through the dot in the centre. As the final rung on the ladder of the planets, the coagulation process, the Sun is recognised as gold – light condensed into physical form and the spiritualization of matter, represented by our hearts and vital force.

In astrology, the regal Sun symbolizes the ego and the expressive self, personal power, creative energy and individual identity through the solar plexus. In its position in a chart, the sun or star sign categorizes the fundamental blueprint for the expression of the soul in that lifetime. The Sun is domicile in Leo, in detriment in Aquarius, exalted in Aries and in fall in Libra. With Leo, it rules the fifth house in astrology of creativity, play and pleasure. The cycle of the Sun is 365 days, and each year it returns to the exact place in the chart as the moment of birth; this is known as a solar return, and is an accurate measure of our birthday. It also corresponds directly to the heart, as our inner sun, and eyesight, as our inner vision (specifically the right eye in men and the left in women), and it distributes the vital force through the circulatory and immune systems. Our alignment to source is reflected in the Sun's rulership of physical uprightness in the spine and back. Excess conditions are heating, drying and inflammatory. Sympathetic remedies will be Sun and Mars plants. In antipathy, we look to cooling and demulcent, anti-inflammatory remedies of the Moon, Venus and Neptune, or the cold, slow and contracting nature of Saturn to balance excess solar forces. Deficient Sun may lead to melancholy and sadness.

The Sun takes a year to pass through the zodiac, so it governs annuals, and yellow and orange plants with round, radiating shapes. Sun plants encourage self-confidence and overall vitality, and are often restorative tonics that support the whole system. Rowan (*Sorbus aucuparia*), also known as mountain ash, is a powerful protective tree of the Sun. It is high in antioxidants and it tones and fortifies the vital force of the body. Ash (*Fraxinus excelsior*) is sacred to the Sun, associated with the Norse Tree of Life, Yggdrasil, connector of worlds. The keys (seed pods) are traditionally pickled, while a tea made from the leaves detoxes the system, acting as a diuretic and laxative. Calendula (*Calendula officinalis*) is a Sun herb, yet it acts on the fire element through the waters of the body. It gently warms and moves the fluids of the lymphatic system, and is a key anti-inflammatory herb. Gorse (*Ulex europaeus*) lifts the spirits, and brings back the sunshine when all hope is lost. Gorse is a hardy shrub that flowers all year round – hence the phrase 'Kissing is out of fashion when the gorse is out of bloom.' Gorse flowers produce a nutty, coconut flavour, which makes them good to wild-nibble on while walking or to use in a syrup. In the language of flowers, gorse represents love for all the seasons. Similarly, St John's wort (*Hypericum perforatum*) holds the solar vibration and its oil is referred to as 'bottled sunshine'. Angelica (*Angelica archangelica*) is a digestive tonic and circulatory stimulant associated with Archangel Michael. It was used extensively in the Middle Ages against 'poison and plague', according to John Gerard's *Herball* – it is effective against fever, colds and flu. Warming and oily, it shifts excess stagnant phlegm, oils and fats. Rosemary (*Rosemary officinalis*) stimulates the metabolism, increasing oxygenation, nutrient intake and the detoxification process. It softly warms and stimulates the blood and the nerves, and supports memory recall. As a conduit of the Sun, it also plays a role in connecting the brain with the intelligence of the heart.

Other examples of plants with solar rulership include acacia, anemone, bay laurel, burnet, cedar, chamomile, daisy, eyebright, frankincense, goldenseal, greater celandine, hawthorn, hazel, juniper, lovage, mistletoe, myrrh, oak, olive, rhodiola, saffron, sunflower, tormentil and walnut.

St John's Wort Summer Solstice Oil

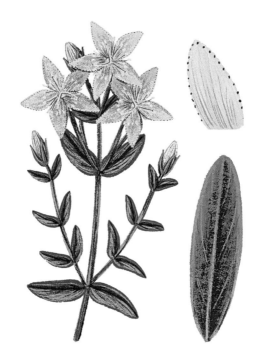

An archetypal sun plant, St John's wort (*Hypericum perforatum,* opposite) is traditionally picked at noon when the Sun is at its zenith on Midsummer's Day (the summer solstice). Calendula (*Calendula officinalis*) is a suitable pairing with this plant.

An energetically protective herb, St John's wort calms the nervous system, and Culpeper recommended a tincture of the flowers 'against melancholy and madness'. *Perforatum* refers to the tiny perforations on the petals that are actually oil glands. This oil is extracted through an oil infusion process that produces a bright red colour and is used to treat wounds (its perforated petals are a signature for wounds and skin rashes). Its astringent properties tonify and dry up excess fluid, and it is an effective liver tonic, which is why it is contraindicated with some medicines as its action on the liver metabolises them before they can be fully absorbed.

Culpeper designated Calendula as a Sun plant under the sign of Leo, and a remedy for strengthening the heart. Calendula means 'little calendar', as it is heliotropic, meaning it traces the sun across the sky from east to west during the day. It is said to bloom every month and foretell the coming of rain if it doesn't open. Applied topically, calendula alleviates and supports the healing of sunburn, minor burns and rashes, or skin ailments due to excess heat or inflammation.

METHOD

1 When greeting St John's wort at midday on the summer solstice, acknowledge the energy exchange between the Sun and the St John's wort, and between the plant and yourself. Consider the relationship of the Sun to all plants and to the planets of our solar system, and honour that light that exists with plants, planets and people. With the same intention, gather the just-opened calendula flower heads in the morning, when the dew has dried. You may use the whole flowers or just the petals, but ensure they are completely dry before making the remedy, as excess moisture will spoil the oil. St John's wort, on the other hand, should not be dried before making the oil, so that it can be extracted from the leaves.

2 Fill a jar with the two types of flowers and cover with sunflower or olive oil.

3 Close the lid and place in a sunny spot for a philosophical month (40 days). Check regularly to ensure that the plant matter is completely covered by the oil.

4 When it is ready, strain to remove the flowers and place the liquid in an amber glass bottle. Store in a cool, dark place. You may wish to add a few drops of vitamin E oil as a preservative.

APPLICATION

Test a little oil on your skin to check for photosensitivity (reaction to UV light). Apply to minor skin ailments or use as a skin serum to soothe and lift the spirits. Dab on pulse points for protection and to connect to the frequency of the Sun.
Caution: For external use only.

Moon

In esoteric law and in modern astronomy, it is thought that the Moon came from the Earth, expelled by another body such as a planet or asteroid, so there is a particular type of shared resonance between the Earth and Moon. The Moon is tidally locked to Earth, and its near side always faces the Earth, so we never fully see the dark side. Lunar forces are represented in our hidden, shadow side, our subconscious and our memories, represented by a semi-circle.

The Moon is receptive and its metal is silver. It has no light itself, only reflecting the light of the Sun out into the cosmos, through its alchemical process of distillation. It takes the raw external conscious energy of the Sun, internalizes it, and dissolves and distils it into a more refined expression. As the closest celestial body to Earth, it receives the rays of all the planets and filters these to Earth. The Moon is the crescent cup that holds our inner waters and reflects them back to us. Where the Sun is an outward expression, the Moon is magnetic, pulling downward and in an inward expression of cosmic consciousness.

In astrology, the position of the Moon in a chart represents the emotional and the subconscious influences, the shadow self and the mother archetype. With Cancer, it rules the fourth house of home. The sign of the zodiac the Moon is in when you are born reflects the areas that might be sensitive to external influences, and how you might adapt to change. The Moon is domicile in Cancer, in detriment in Capricorn, exalted in Taurus and in fall in Scorpio. The Moon rules the waters of the body and the flow of fluids and electromagnetic currents; it guides the tides of the sea and the inner tides of the female menstruation cycle. Cold and moist by nature, it governs the fluids of the brain, the lymphatic system and the stomach. Sympathetic plants are ruled by the Moon, Venus and Neptune, correlating to the waters of the body, with milky saps and soothing mucilages such as poppy (*Papaver rhoeas*) and aloe vera (*Aloe barbadensis miller*). If there are excess lunar forces, causing swelling or leaking of the fluids in the body, or

damp stagnation, these can be channelled with lunar lymphatics or remedied with the drying heat of Sun and Mars plants, or given boundaries via Saturn.

The lunar nodes describe the relationship between the path of the Sun and Moon. The line that the Sun draws in the sky from the position of the Earth is called the ecliptic. The Moon follows a separate path, and the points where this path crosses that of the solar ecliptic are called the north and south nodes, which are key points in astrology. The north node represents those qualities that we are drawn towards, entangled with our soul's purpose and growth. It causes an excess of energy, associated with abscesses and the accumulation of toxins. The south node has a draining, diffusive nature, and its position in the chart can indicate areas where energy leaks out, causing weakness and fatigue. It is associated with malnourishment, addiction and mental illness.

The Moon takes on average 28 days to orbit Earth, so governs the germination of seeds. Lunar plants are often water-dwelling, oily with succulent leaves and white or purple in colour. Lunaria (*Lunaria annua*) or moonwort, meaning 'moon-shaped', gets its name from its silicles (pods), which appear as translucent silvery discs. For this reason, it is also called honesty, silver dollar and money plant. In modern medicine, it has been used in the treatment of multiple sclerosis due to high levels of nervonic acid (mono-unsaturated Omega 9), which nourishes the brain. Willow (*Salix alba*) grows by water and once gave its name to Helicon, the abode of nine muses who were orgiastic priestesses of the moon goddess. It reflects back the cold and moist conditions of the phlegmatic lunar forces through its cold and dry astringent action. The cooling and moisturizing properties of chickweed (*Stellaria media*) as a bath or poultice soothe skin conditions and inflammation.

Other plants with lunar signatures include birch, camphor, chasteberry, cleavers, lady's mantle, lady's smock, lotus, mallow, milky oats, moonflower, mugwort, purslane, rockrose, watercress, water lily, poppies, white roses and wild lettuce.

Poppy
Sleep Elixir

Sleep and dreaming lie under the guidance of the Moon. Field poppy (*Papaver rhoeas*) has the lunar signature of milky sap and contains lactucarium, which has a similar effect to the opium poppy. It can be used as a mild sedative, for pain relief, and as a sleep aid, sympathetic to the Moon's governance of the fluids of the brain.

A relative of the opium poppy (*Papaver somniferum*), whose name comes from the Latin *somnus*, meaning 'sleep', this plant does not contain morphine, but is antispasmodic and mildly sedative, so is traditionally used for its calming effect. In Homer's *Odyssey*, he writes that poppy was added to wine 'to lull all pain and anger and bring forgetfulness of every sorrow'.

Energetically, it disperses anxiety and fear, fostering courage and confidence. Poppies are associated with the liminal realms, altered states of consciousness, and Hypnos, the god of sleep, and Morpheus, the god of dreams. The milk of field poppy contains similar alkaloids to that of the opium poppy, but in a fractional quantity. It is not narcotic or addictive, and the petals are used in folk remedies as a sudorific and to reduce fever and alleviate coughs. Poppies are associated with memory and death, growing out of the disturbed soils of battlefields, thought to spring from the blood of wounded soldiers. In the language of flowers, the common poppy symbolizes consolation, remembrance and temperance, and means 'I will not allow myself to be rushed.' In the nineteenth century laudanum, a tincture made from opium poppies, became popular with the Romantic poets.

METHOD

1 Gather field poppy petals on a full moon, ideally before dawn when the dew is still moist on the plants. A well-placed Neptune or Pisces moon may aid in dream magic.

2 Separate the red poppy petals from the flower head, ensuring no black stamens remain, as these will affect the colour of the elixir. Place them into a glass jar and cover with brandy and 1 teaspoon of raw local honey.

3 Add a few drops of crystal essences with an aligned purpose for sleep and dreaming, such as selenite, amethyst, blue howlite and unakite.

4 Leave for one lunar phase, stirring intermittently and ensuring the plant matter is covered. The liquid will turn a reddish pink and purple.

APPLICATION

Take 1 teaspoon at night before bed or add to hot water for a warm infusion. Make a dream intention before you sleep.

Mercury

Mercury is the smallest and fastest planet in our solar system and closest to the Sun, completing its orbit in just 88 days and acting as a transmitter and messenger of solar rays to the rest of the solar system. It can be seen pre-dawn on the eastern horizon. Mercury's glyph contains spirit, soul and body, reflecting its ability to mediate and unify soul and matter through spirit. Mercury transitions and evolves the process of fermentation into distillation, drawing up the ferment of the imagination into the heavens to be distilled down into matter.

The energetics of Mercury correspond to the air element in the astrological chart, as well as expansion and contraction, movement and change, intellect, thought, writing and speech. Mercury or quicksilver is a powerful neurotoxin, and its ability to move and change rapidly is reflective of Mercury's inherent energetics. The quick-witted messenger god, Mercury rules the airwaves and all methods of communication, technology, travel and trade. Mercury is domicile in Gemini and Virgo, in detriment in Sagittarius and Pisces, exalted in Virgo and in fall in Pisces. With Gemini, it rules the third house of communication and sharing, and with Virgo, the sixth house of work, service and health.

Mercury is known for its retrograde cycles. This is when the planet appears as if it is stationary or moving backwards in the sky. This happens three or four times per year, and causes disruption to travel and communication. However, as is the nature of all retrograde cycles, it is a valuable time to reflect and review rather than take action: a necessary pause in the year. The sign that the retrograde is in will influence the quality of the time – for example, if Mercury is retrograde in Libra, it is time to review the balance of our relationships and homeostasis within our bodies and our environment. Mercury governs the air element in the body, the nervous and respiratory systems, along with the neural connections of the brain and the pineal gland. It influences the communication channels of speech and hearing. The hermaphrodite psychopomp moving between worlds, Mercury shifts our cellular vibration, changing the direction and flow of electromagnetic currents in our nerve fibres. Through Gemini, it governs pairs in the body and twins. The placement of Mercury in a chart influences our ability to communicate and negotiate. It is cold and dry in nature, and any excess can call for antispasmodics, nervines and expectorants, the moistening and relaxing remedies of the Moon and Venus, or the grounding qualities of the earth element.

Mercurial plants have air signatures of hollow stems or spaced delicate leaves, and are airy or spindly in nature. Fennel (*Foeniculum vulgare*) is a good representative of this. It acts as a digestive and carminative, releasing trapped gas from the digestive tract. Mint, such as peppermint (*Mentha × piperita*), water mint (*Mentha aquatica*) and spearmint (*Mentha spicata*), is a herb of Mercury, with its ability to both stimulate and relax, and to ease nerve and stress conditions relating to digestion. Liquorice (*Glycyrrhiza glabra*) supports mercurial functions in that it calms the nervous system and soothes the digestive and respiratory systems. The morphology of the lion's mane fungi (*Hericium erinaceus*) bears a resemblance to the brain and nerve fibres, and it is primarily used to repair nerve damage and support brain health.

Other examples of plants with mercurial qualities include caraway, chaparral, clover, coffee, common germander, dill, Douglas fir, elecampane, ginkgo, gotu kola, hazel, honeysuckle, horehound, linden, liquorice, lungwort, mahonia, marjoram, mulberry, oregano, parsley, pine, red clover, savory, Scots pine, thyme, valerian, vervain, walnut and wild carrot.

Lavender Hydrosol

Lavender (*Lavandula angustifolia*) is a nervine and relaxant plant used to aid anxiety, headaches and nervous tension. Thought to protect from evil, its antimicrobial and antibacterial properties were employed against the plague, and its essential oils were used to ward off insects.

It is a sedative, anti-convulsive and mood-stablising herb. Culpeper says of lavender: 'Mercury owns this herb. It is of special use in the pains of the head and brain which proceed from cold ... or sluggish malady, cramps, convulsions, and often faintings.' Its purple flowers and scent are associated with the crown and purity of the higher mind. In Egypt, it was used in the embalming process to purify the soul (its name is derived from the Latin *lavare*, meaning 'to wash'). Energetically, it works to remove mental blockages. Hildegard von Bingen wrote of lavender's cleansing powers of a spiritual and energetic nature: 'It curbs very many evil things and, because of it, malign spirits are terrified.' In the language of flowers, lavender represents serenity and devotion.

METHOD

1 On Mercury's day (Wednesday), gather lavender sprigs. Hydrosols require approximately 10 cups of water per cup of plant material. After washing the lavender, steep in filtered cold water for 3 hours before you begin. This is the saucepan method.

2 Nestle a small bowl in the centre of the pot. The hydrosol bowl should be separate from the lavender water, so you may need to raise the bowl by placing an upside-down bowl or strainer beneath it.

3 Heat the water. When it begins to simmer, turn the lid of the saucepan upside down. The steam will rise to the lid and condense, and then this condensation (the hydrosol) will drip down and collect in the bowl at the centre of the pan. Place some ice on top of the upturned lid – this will cool the hot vapour, condensing it faster.

4 Continue for around 30 minutes, or until you have collected sufficient hydrosol. Producing essential oils requires a very large amount of matter and an alembic still, but you may be able to skim off any oil that appears on the surface using a cotton bud.

5 Cool the hydrosol and decant into spritz bottles.

APPLICATION

Spray a mist of the hydrosol around you when you need to disperse anxiety or just before you go to sleep. Culpeper recommends taking it for 'tremblings and passions of the heart, and faintings and swooning'. Alternatively, soak a cloth with the hydrosol and place in the fridge to cool, then use as a compress to be placed over the eyes and temple.

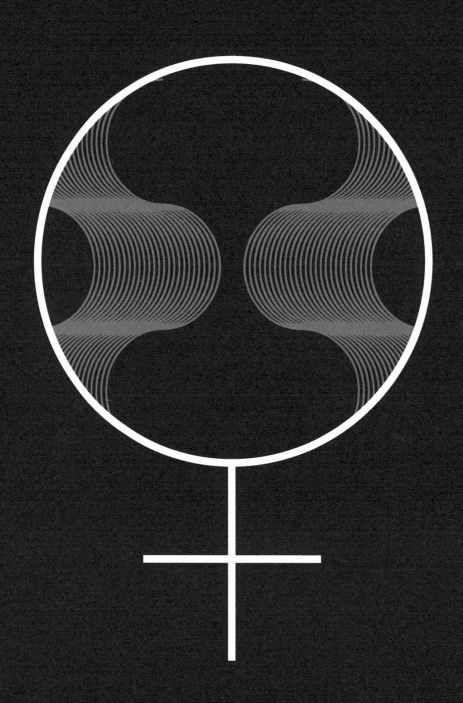

Venus

Venus is the brightest planet and appears as a morning star in the east just before dawn or as the evening star in the west just after sunset. The glyph for Venus places a cross below the circle, representing the spirit having dominion over matter. Its metal is highly conductive and malleable copper. Venus is an astrological benefic, meaning that its qualities are primarily beneficial. Venus is abundant in nature and a force of attraction, channelling spirit into matter, embodying the higher virtues of cosmic and divine love into the physical. The alchemical marriage of the conjunction stage is the union of these dual aspects. Venus strives for harmonic balance, and governs desires and the manifestation of these desires into reality or the physical body, delighting in sensual pleasures and corresponding with creative expression, romance, love, sex and the arts. The glyph may also be perceived as a mirror holding a reflection to our self-image, self-love and self-worth, and also reflects how in a relationship, the other person holds a mirror to ourselves and our behaviour.

Energetically, Venus wishes to balance relationships, and physiologically it does this through the kidneys, urinary tract, and female sexual organs and fertility. Venus is domicile in Taurus and Libra, in detriment in Scorpio and Aries, exalted in Pisces and in fall in Virgo. With Taurus, it rules the second house of material goods and value, and with Libra, the seventh house of love, relationships and partnership. Venus influences beauty through the appearance of skin, hair and lips, and balances through the thymus gland. When Venus is in excess, fluids build up, causing damp and stagnation, requiring similar fluid remedies that flush the lymphatic system, or the warming and drying remedies of the Sun and Mars, or the boundary conditions of Saturn.

Many plants by nature of their beauty have an affiliation with Venus. Plants with a strong Venus correspondence are attractive, smooth and fragrant, often five-petalled and fruit-bearing, with colours of white, pink and indigo, and are of a sensual nature. They are often diuretics and demulcent, working on the female reproductive system and as aphrodisiacs. Rose (*Rosa spp.*) is the archetypal plant of Venus, mirrored in the Rose of Venus (see page 6). According to Culpeper, red roses and roseships belong to Jupiter, white roses to the Moon and damask roses to Venus. Rose governs the inner waters of the heart and womb. It is astringent and cooling, navigating excesses of water and soothing. It is also a sensual aphrodisiac, nervine and nourishing relaxant. Energetically, it opens the heart, lifts the spirits and embraces with compassion and gentleness while retaining its integrity and purpose through clarity and discernment. Its thorns are its tool of discernment, and they can pierce the heart of an issue to reveal the truth. Its essence allows beauty to be seen in the world again after trauma.

Pasqueflower (*Pulsatilla vulgaris*), meaning 'passover', corresponds to Easter and the spring equinox, and is an antispasmodic and nervine that relaxes the nervous and reproductive systems. Paracelsus once asked, 'What is Venus but the *Artemisia* in your garden?' This is in reference to the *Artemisia* family, which includes wormwood (*Artemisia absinthium*) and mugwort (*Artemisia vulgaris*), each of which has the potential to support the hearts of those that are triumphing out of chaos or trauma. Artemis is the huntress who guarded the forest, women and childbirth. Venus rules the veins, and so relates to the qualities of horse chestnut (*Aesculus hippocastanum*) and witch hazel (*Hamamelis virginiana*), which have a direct effect on strengthening blood vessels and draining excess fluids.

Other plants that correspond to Venus include alder, apple, artichoke, chaste tree, chasteberry, cleavers, daisy, damiana, elder, feverfew, ginkgo, heather, honeysuckle, lady's bedstraw, lady's slipper, lady's mantle, lemon balm, lemon verbena, linden, mallows, meadowsweet, motherwort, nipplewort, passionflower, pennyroyal, pomegranate, primrose, pulsatilla, red clover, red raspberry, rose, self-heal, thyme, uva ursi, verbena, vervain and wood sorrel.

Lady's Mantle
and Rose Glycerite

Lady's mantle (*Alchemilla vulgaris*) is considered to be the alchemist plant, with its name translating as 'little alchemist'. Culpeper said of it: 'Venus claims the herb as her own.'

It produces a dew from its internal laboratory that collects in the funnel of its leaves, and this magical elixir is said to hold the secret to transmute any alchemical formula, cure all disease and invoke great beauty. The excretion of the water is a process known as guttation, which occurs in humid conditions when the soil is moist and the air cool and damp. At night the stomata (leaf pores) close, but the roots continue to take up water, building pressure. It is this pressure that pushes the water droplets to be released through pores on the leaf margins called hydathodes. Paracelsus described the vehicle for cosmic influences to act upon physical matter as the archaeus – the *anima mundi* that communicates the heavens and the soul to the planet and body. Paracelsus called the dew produced by lady's mantle, 'celestial water', a pure and direct emanation of the heavens on Earth.

This plant has strong earth goddess energy that relates to Venus and Freya, though it is particularly aligned with the Virgin Mary. It was even thought to restore lost virginity. In the body, it tonifies the tissues and calms the nerves, and as a uterine tonic and hormone balancer, it covers a wide range of gynaecological complaints, acting on all parts of the female reproductive system. Energetically, it is linked to fertility magic, protects childbirth and opens up the third eye.

METHOD

1 On a Friday (Venus's day) morning, just before sunrise, collect the sacred dew directly from the tips of the lady's mantle leaves, either using a pipette or by placing a thin cotton handkerchief over the leaf to absorb the dew, then wringing it out. This is a vibrational remedy, so you only require a small amount.

2 Gather some of the lady's mantle leaves and also some of wild dog rose petals.

3 Make an essence of the dew by adding it directly into a bottle of spring or distilled water, blending with vodka in a 1:1 ratio for your tincture.

4 Place the washed lady's mantle leaves in a pan and cover with water. Put the lid on and gently simmer for 5 minutes (in honour of the five petals of the Rose of Venus).

5 Remove from the heat and leave to steep with the lid on for eight hours (to honour the eight-year cycle of the orbit). Add at least double the amount of glycerin to the liquid, ensuring all plant matter is well covered, and leave in a cool dark place for one lunar phase, agitating every few days. Strain through muslin into a glass bottle, and add a few drops of the lady's mantle essence.

APPLICATION

Take 1 teaspoon when you need to call upon the energetics of love, healing and protection. It may be beneficial at the beginning of your moon cycle or on a full moon for non-menstruating people to connect to the energy of heaven on earth, the goddess frequencies and the inner alchemist within. This essence opens the heart and transcends barriers.

Mars

Mars, known as the red planet, is the archetypal warrior, the god of war and the dynamic yang and masculine expression that is reflected in the metallic correspondence of iron. It is recognizable in the sky due to its unique red glow due to high levels of iron oxide. Whereas Venus channels spirit into matter, Mars forces spirit from matter, and this is depicted in the cross of fixed earth that sits on top of the circle of spirit in the glyph. In astrology, this glyph was adapted to depict an arrow, representing the dynamic warrior energy moving up and out from spirit. It shows an outward movement of the vital force and the expressive energy of Mars. Its alchemical act is separation, driven by force and determination. Mars fights for what it believes in, leaving all else behind. Iron rusts through oxidation, and so on the psycho-spiritual journey, we come into contact with new information and perspectives, transforming our nature so that we detach from our old selves.

Mars corresponds with the fire element mythologically and to the ego forces and iron in our blood. But in reality, Mars is a cold, dry desert, though it may not always have been this way. Mars qualities are ego, will, instinct and action. Mars is considered a malefic planet in that its presence can cause conflict, but it is also a call to action and vital source of energy that propels our visions forwards. Mars is domicile in Aries and Scorpio, in detriment in Libra and Taurus, exalted in Capricorn and in fall in Cancer. With Aries, it rules the first house of the self and identity, and with Scorpio and Pluto, the eighth house of death and transformation.

Mars rules the iron in the blood and the adrenals, gallbladder, immune response, and male sexual hormones and virility. Mars energetics are hot and dry, stimulating and activating. Its placement in the astrological chart can relate to areas of physical and psycho-spiritual inflammation. Mars is met with the stimulating and fortifying remedies it rules, and can also benefit from cooling bitters and anti-inflammatories, soothed by remedies of the Moon or Venus.

Mars passes through the zodiac about every two years, so it governs biennials. Mars plants have signatures of thorns, red colouring, upwards energy and stimulating properties. They may cause stinging or irritation, such as nettles (*Urtica dioica*). Hawthorn (*Crataegus monogyna*) bears the thorns, red berries and morphology of Mars, and its primary action is on the blood and heart as a circulatory tonic. However, it does not share the quickening nature of Mars. Instead, it is usually necessary to take hawthorn for at least three months, as it is a slow-acting, slow-building herb, and this allows it to go deep. This is also a useful signature for Mars types to avoid burnout, and acts as a reminder to take things slowly and assuredly. Yellow dock (*Rumex crispus*) is high in iron and supports the absorption of the mineral. As a bitter alterative, it purifies the blood and stimulates bile in the liver and gallbladder. It cools excess heat and inflammation of Mars. Ginger (*Zingiber officinale*) stimulates and warms the system and is a good source of iron.

Basil (*Ocimum basilicum*) is a herb of Mars. With its pungent smell, it used to heal stings and bites, and also as a strewing herb to offer protection from enemies and entities. Piperine in black pepper (*Piper nigrum*) is anti-inflammatory and supports the increase of bile, gallbladder function and reduction in stones, particularly when combined with turmeric (*Curcum longa*). Rosebay willowherb (*Chamerion angustifolium*) has been used in the treatment of the prostate.

Other examples of plants with Mars influences include astragalus, barberry, beech, blessed thistle, bryonia, butcher's broom, cacti, cayenne, common boneset, daffodil, dragon's blood, garlic, gentian, gorse, holly, hops, horseradish, jack-by-the-hedge, juniper, lesser celandine, osha, pineappleweed, sarsaparilla, sea buckthorn, thistle, usnea, wild rocket, woodruff and wormwood.

Nettle Beer

A key Mars plant is nettle (*Urtica dioica*), with its signature sting from the presence of tiny hair-spears containing formic acid. Nettle is highly nutritive, containing many trace minerals, and is high in both iron and vitamin C, which helps with iron absorption and alleviates adrenal fatigue.

Nettle builds the proteins in the blood and supports metabolic processes. As a diuretic and anti-inflammatory, it is cooling and relieves the body of excess Mars heat and activity. Culpeper noted that, as a herb of Mars, nettles are hot and dry, and thus consuming them in spring was a good antidote to the phlegmatic 'cold and wet that winter hath left behind' in the body. Urtication is the practice of self-flaggelation or rubbing with nettle stings, and is used as a treatment for inflammatory conditions such as arthritis. Energetically, it brings us into the present moment and redefines excess watery emotions to give new life and purpose. In the language of flowers, nettles are said to mean 'you are hateful', and to represent anger, slander and intolerance. The nettle's stinging hairs and ability to cause harm also gave it the badge of protection, guarding against demons and giving it the common name Devil's wort.

Nettle is also one of the plants of the Anglo-Saxon Nine Herbs Charm, recorded in the *Lacnunga* manuscript in the 10th century AD, along with others including mugwort, plantain and chamomile. The herbs were combined into a paste and administered to the wound, while the charm was incanted into the mouth and ears of the patient.

METHOD

1 On a Tuesday, just before sunrise or on the hour of Mars (see page 44), fill your basket with young nettle tops.
2 Wash them with gloves on, and then place them in a large pot. Fill to the top with water. For around 1 kg nettle tops, you'll need 5 litres water.
3 Bring to the boil and add 1 teaspoon of Irish moss (to break down the proteins that cloud the beer), then simmer until the water goes dark green (this will take around 20 minutes).
4 If you like, you could now strain and save the nettle tops to calcify them in order to create a spagyric advancement of this recipe (see pages 100 and 178). Add sugar to the pot (about 500 g sugar for 1 kg nettle tops), and stir until combined, then allow to cool.
5 Transfer into a sterilized fermentation bucket with a bung and airlock, and add the juice of 2 lemons and 1 teaspoon active yeast powder.
6 Monitor every few days. Mars's orbit is 687 days, and the beer will be ready on or around day 6, 7 or 8, although you may leave it for longer for a deeper brew.
7 Siphon into sterilized bottles, avoiding the sediment at the bottom. Time will mature the brew.

APPLICATION
Drink in moderation for fortification.

Jupiter

Jupiter is the largest planet in our solar system, and rests just beyond the asteroid belt. It is the fourth brightest celestial object, just behind Venus, and shines brighter than Mars or Saturn. The giant red spot at its centre is a storm larger than Earth that has been raging for more than a century. In esoteric lore, this is seen to represent the war of the gods. The glyph for Jupiter is the crescent soul elevated above the cross of matter, with the quality of expansion and radiance. This is a representation of our vital force moving up and out beyond the boundaries of physical matter, and signifies connecting to the spiritual component of our reality. The alchemical metal associated with the gaseous Jupiter is the lightweight tin, and the expansive, exaggerated quality of Jupiter assists in the dissolution stage.

Jupiter is known as 'the Great Benefic', and represents legal and religious matters, trade, good fortune, and growth and expansion. Its energetics can be hot and moist or cold and moist. Jupiter is domicile in Sagittarius and Pisces, in detriment in Gemini and Virgo, exalted in Cancer and in fall in Capricorn. With Sagittarius, it rules the ninth house of higher learning and philosophy. The jovial spirit of Jupiter can lead to excess and overindulgence, causing obesity and stagnation, addiction and states of excess growth. Jupiter rules the pituitary gland, arterial circulation, the liver and the metabolism, and plays a digestive role through the breakdown of fat. Remedies often required for Jupiter imbalance call for mercurial bitters and tonics, such as remedies for liver congestion and wind tension, Mars and Sun circulatory stimulants, and Lunar and Venusian diuretics to filter the lymphatic system and eliminate waste. Saturn's action is to reign in Jupiter, creating tone and structure.

A Jovian (Jupiter) year is twelve years, which synchronizes with the life cycle of perennials. Jupiter plants often have the signature of a cross and were later named *Cruciferae* by Linnaeus. They are often nutritive and abundant in fruits and nuts, large in stature, and can be found in colours of blue, indigo, yellow and orange. Figs are a quintessentially Jovian plant. A symbol of sexuality, Jupiter has an estimated 79 moons, many named after his endless lovers. Fig leaf (*Ficus lyrata* or *Ficus carica*) is used to treat diabetes and high cholesterol, while figs themselves help ease constipation. Linden (*Tilia* × *vulgaris*), also known as the lime tree, is a mild sedative, relaxant, antispasmodic and nervine herb that diffuses tension. Linden tea is taken for anxiety, insomnia and tension headaches. Its heart-shaped leaves are an indication in the doctrine of signatures for its use as a cardiotonic, lowering high blood pressure and cholesterol. Other Jupiter plant allies are dandelion (*Taraxacum officinale*) and burdock (*Arctium lappa*), bitter alteratives and diuretics that act on the liver, gallbladder and kidneys to purify the blood. Milk thistle (*Silybum marianum*) is another key liver herb, and contains trace elements of Jupiter's metal, tin. Oak (*Quercus robur*), like Jupiter, is considered King of the Trees and the Tree of Life, and is associated in many cosmologies with gods of thunder and lightning. Acorns are nutritive, and protect the heart, and are emblems of good luck and protection, particularly from lightning. Grape (*Vitis vinifera*) is a jovial plant that Dioscorides recommended to improve the appetite, relieve stomach pains and halt diarrhoea, and can be used in the form of wine to reduce a fever. Oregon grape (*Mahonia aquifolium*) is high in antioxidants, hepatoprotective (protects the liver) and anti-inflammatory, and is traditionally used to treat indigestion, gout and rheumatic conditions.

Other examples of plants with jovial signatures include agrimony, alexanders, almond, angelica, anise, arnica, bay, beechnut, bilberries, birch, borage, chervil, chestnut, cinquefoil, dock, henbane, hyssop, jasmine, lady's smock, magnolia, marjoram, mastic, meadowsweet, mulberry, nutmeg, pine, samphire, sweet cicely, vervain, white cedar, wood avens and wood betony.

Lemon
Balm Spagyric

Lemon balm (*Melissa officinalis*) is sacred to Jupiter. Paracelsus described this aromatic plant as the 'elixir of life' on account of its multi-dimensional healing properties.

It is a calming nervine that eases anxiety and balances moods, soothing the heart and acting as a strong aid to someone prone to panic attacks. A joyful plant that is a symbol of abundance, it lifts the spirits and restores vitality, sharing Jupiter's jovial nature. Galen praised it for stabilising moods and anxiety, and Avicenna recommended it as an anti-depressant. An eau de mélisse known as Carmelite Water, made by Carmelite nuns, has lemon balm as a primary ingredient, combined with other aromatic herbs. To Culpeper, it 'causeth the mind and heart to become merry, and reviveth the heart fainting to foundlings, especially of such who are overtaken in their sleep, and driveth away all troublesome cares and thought'. Energetically, it attracts love, and in the language of flowers, it represents sympathy, wisdom, compassion and virtue. The genus name *Melissa* comes from the Greek for honeybee, and this plant is sacred to bees. Pliny the Elder wrote: 'Bees are delighted with this herbe above all others … when they are straid away, they do finde their way home againe by it.'

METHOD

1 Around the new moon, gather lemon balm leaves and stems before flowering and dry the plant.

2 Crush the plant in a mortar with a pestle, holding the intention for your remedy in your mind. Place in a glass jar and seal the lid.

3 While the moon is waxing, pour vodka over the plant matter until it is well covered.

4 Place in a dark place at room temperature until the Moon is full.

5 On Jupiter's day, strain the liquid into a dark glass bottle.

6 Put the plant matter into a crucible or ceramic pot and heat until it chars. This should be done outside. Once cooled, grind the burnt plant to a powder with a pestle and mortar.

7 Return to the heat until it turns to a fine grey-white ash.

8 Once cooled, cover with distilled or filtered spring water. Cover and gently simmer for 20 minutes, then boil for 12 minutes.

9 Allow to cool and filter through a cheesecloth before returning the liquid to the cleaned pot. Simmer until the liquid begins to evaporate, leaving only the salts.

10 Continue to heat the salts in the pot with the lid on until they become a pure white.

11 Place the purified salts in a sealed jar.

12 At Jupiter's hour, slowly add the tincture to the salts and hermetically seal. Place in a dark place at room temperature for one lunar cycle.

APPLICATION

Take a few drops on the tongue as required.

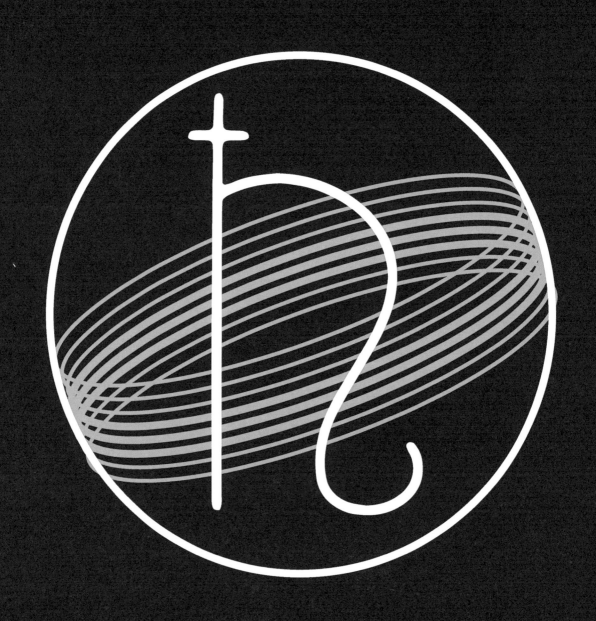

Saturn

Saturn is best viewed when in opposition – which occurs every 378 days, when Earth passes between it and the Sun. When this happens, it is brightest in the sky, rising in the east and setting to the west. Its glyph is the reverse of Jupiter's, with matter presiding over the soul. Saturn is 'the Lord of Time' (after the Greek Cronos), and comes from the Latin *serere*, meaning 'to sow of plant' – *to manifest*. It resides over karma, death and transformation.

At the edge of the solar system, we see Saturn as the grand cosmic gatekeeper to the physical. It is the archetype of the spiritualization of matter, and in esoteric lore, any new levels of consciousness entering from outside of our solar system – as comets or asteroids with extra-terrestrial DNA – must first be received by Saturn's force, making it the judge of human progression and giving birth to evolution. In this sense, Saturn is thought to guard the ancestral realm. The metal associated with Saturn is lead, the densest of the metals at the lowest rung of the ladder of the planets, representing the ego, bound by the conditioned self. The nature of Saturn is contraction, a downwards and inwards motion of limitation. It is cold and dry by nature, and this boundary force is reflected in the morphology of its icy rings.

Known as 'the Great Malefic', Saturn's teachings offer profound transformation, but require that we face our shadows head-on to transmute our own boundaries and limitations. When Saturn first returns to transit the natal chart in the same position it was in at our birth, every 28–30 years, we often experience the dark night of the soul. In alchemy, Saturn is considered the beginning and the end of the Great Work, when we must offer to the flames what is no longer serving us. It is the initial stage of calcination, when the leaden and dross qualities of Saturn must be transformed through fire. All possibilities exist within the darkness of Saturn, and from this state of putrefaction, the light of Albedo will emerge from the dark (see page 18). Saturn is domicile in Capricorn and Aquarius, in detriment in Cancer and Leo, exalted in Libra and in fall in Aries. With Capricorn,

it rules the tenth house of career and ambition. Saturn desires structure, order and strong ethics and values. It tempers and balances the planets, reflected in its exaltation in Libra, the scales of the zodiac.

Saturn rules the spleen, bones, musculoskeletal system and teeth. It causes contraction, tension and the slowing down of metabolic functions, restricting flow in the body and also a build-up of matter such as stones. Saturn deficiencies need Jupiter's nutritive expansive remedies, Mars and the Sun to warm the digestive system and break down rigidity and stagnation, and the Moon and Venus to lubricate the joints and oils in the body. Saturn deficiencies benefit from anodynes, circulatory stimulants, nutritive tonics, carminatives, antispasmodics, demulcents and relaxants.

Saturn influences woody perennials, where the slow growth of heavy substance is revealed by growth rings that in turn mirror the rings of Saturn. Saturn plant remedies are astringent and cooling, nutritive and grounding. Often, their colours are mottled dark green, brown, and purples, which includes many poisonous plants such as hemlock and deadly nightshade.

Comfrey (*Symphytum officinale*) is a plant of Saturn, a primary ingredient in salves for the skin and bones. Guelder rose (*Viburnum opulus*) supports Saturn in its traditional use, earning its common name of crampbark. Mullein (*Verbascum thapsus*) is a demulcent, cooling herb for relieving dryness, particularly in the respiratory and musculoskeletal systems. Horsetail (*Equisetum arvense*) bears the ring signature of Saturn and corresponds to the physical form in its high silica content and action on strengthening the connective tissues, hair, skin and nails.

Other examples of plants with Saturn energetics are balm of gilead, barley, birdsfoot trefoil, bistort, blackberry, black hellebore, boneset, buttercup, foxglove, fumitory, ground elder, ground ivy, herb gerarde, ivy, medlar, monkshood, moss, pansies, plantain, red cedar and oak (both of which contain traces of lead), rosebay willowherb, Solomon's seal, St John's wort, valerian, wild campion, wintergreen and yew.

Guelder Rose Oxymel

Guelder rose (*Viburnum opulus*) has a long history of use in the treatment of rheumatic conditions, and is also used to relieve muscle cramping and spasms in the lungs, intestine and uterus.

It has a prominent place in Ukrainian folklore and Slavic paganism, where it is associated with the birth of the universe, and the marriage of the trinity of the Sun, the Moon and the stars. It has the feminine energy of the crone, mirroring Cronos, Saturn, and is associated with the passing of time and the festival of Samhain, celebrating death and rebirth. Later versions of the Druid Ogham calendar, an ancient tree calendar of Great Britain, place the period Peith from 28 October to 24 November, under the guardianship of the guelder rose.

The red of the berries of guelder rose may symbolize the fire within the calcination process, as it moves through the stuck and contracted parts within us, stalking and transforming the lower ego and, in doing so, opening up the connection of spirit and soul through the cosmic tryptic of the solar, lunar and celestial forces. The berries, when dried, turn black and were once crushed to make ink.

As an antispasmodic, it was used in folk medicine to treat epilepsy and asthma. Energetically, it relieves areas of mental cramping or tension, and encourages flow.

METHOD

1 On Saturday (Saturn's day), seek a willing tree and make an offering of honey before removing the bark. Use a small knife to remove short strips, ensuring you don't take too much from any branch – and never strip it all the way around. You only need approximately 1 tablespoon per cup.

2 Dry the bark for 3 days or until brittle, then chop and grind it with a pestle and mortar. Place the pieces of bark you have harvested into a small saucepan and add enough water to just allow them to float.

3 Bring to the boil and boil for 7 minutes. Simmer for 7 minutes (the main number of rings Saturn has), and finally let steep for another 7 minutes. The liquid should have reduced slightly and be red-orange in colour.

4 Strain and combine the liquid with an equal part vodka.

5 Add a blend of equal parts honey and raw apple cider vinegar to match the quantity of liquid.

6 Pour the liquid into a glass jar, then add the strips of bark, making sure the liquid covers them before sealing.

7 Seal and leave in a cool, dark place for 29 days (Saturn's orbit is 29 years).

APPLICATION

Take 1 teaspoon when required to alleviate cramping.
Caution: Guelder rose leaves and raw berries are toxic.

Chiron

Chiron was discovered in 1977 at a time when alternative and indigenous wisdom and healing practices were infiltrating popular Western culture. Originally classed as an asteroid, it is now considered to be a comet and a minor planet. Chiron was a wise centaur (half-man, half-horse), alchemist and master healer. He is referred to as 'the wounded healer', as he was shot by Heracles with an arrow dipped in the poisoned blood of the monster-serpent Hydra. In eternal agony, he traded his immortality in return for a final act of altruism: the liberation of Prometheus, who himself had spent an eternity having his liver pecked by a crow each day, only to have it regenerate overnight and the process repeated ad infinitum. Initially defined as an asteroid, Chiron has no rulerships assigned to it. Chiron's glyph is a monogram of the letters O and K (for 'Object Kowal', a provisional name for the object from its discoverer, Charles T. Kowal). Chiron's glyph is also a key, as he provides the wisdom and insight to unlock and access the parts of us that are locked away, and in doing so, open the door to the universe.

Chiron moves between the visible and invisible planets, moving in an elliptical pattern from Uranus down into Saturn and back. Chiron was born of Cronos (Saturn) and was liberator of Prometheus (Uranus). Rejected by the former, he teaches us to move beyond our own suffering, and beyond the conditioned states of family and community, to carve our own path. Chiron has the ability to materialize and dematerialize, moving from spirit to physical realms to gather medicine and wisdom, and brings it back into the material world in order to transform and heal. Chiron's orbit takes around 50 years – and its transit in the natal chart brings around an opportunity for deep fears and core wounds that we have been carrying for a long time to heal. In many ways, Chiron represents the alchemist. He is our great teacher of wisdom and the healing arts, and was the teacher of Asclepius, the Greek god of medicine. Without traditional placements, we might consider Chiron to be domicile in Virgo, influencing the sixth house of health and service. This would make it in detriment in Pisces. As the centaur, it also relates to a Sagittarius exaltation, making it in fall in Gemini. Chiron's placement in a chart is an aspect of healing the parts of our trauma that run deepest, inviting us to the transcendental alchemical process. To transform, we first must see what we are working with. In order to heal and be of service to others, we must first heal ourselves.

In Greek mythology, centaury (*Centaurium erythraea*) and cornflower (*Centaurea cyanus*) are flowers that Chiron used to detox the poison from his wound. Both have bitter principles, acting on the liver and kidneys to purify the blood. Plants used to extract poison or treat snake bites also have a Chiron signature, for example turmeric (*Curcuma longa*), garlic (*Allium sativum*) and oregano (*Origanum vulgare*) and sensitive plant (*Mimosa pudica*), along with wild ginger (*Asarum canadense*). Elecampane (*Inula helenium*) supports elimination of toxins. Greek scholar Theophrastus described it as 'Chiron's panacea'. Yarrow (*Achillea millefolium*) is classically ruled by Venus, but is named after the warrior Achilles, who was said to carry it into battle to staunch wounds. It is also used for psychic protection and is an excellent wound herb. The wounded warrior archetype of yarrow mirrors the wounded healer of Chiron. Yarrow is a shapeshifter plant that can facilitate many actions, and is often seemingly contradictory, such as being both a sedative and a stimulant. Self-heal (*Prunella vulgaris*) is another plant which corresponds to Chiron in its traditional usage as a panacea and its energetic ability to awaken a healing journey within an individual.

Other plants corresponding to Chiron include ashwagandha, chaparral, echinacea, feverfew, goldenseal, grapeseed and parsley.

Self-heal
and Cornflower
Hydrosol

Self-heal (*Prunella vulgaris*) is a soothing plant ally with a history as a cure-all for all manner of ailments. It is a restorative, antiseptic, antiviral, calming and cooling anti-inflammatory used to strengthen the immune system and relieve hypertension.

It is also a lymphatic herb for female complaints. It can be used for lung and digestive issues and as a general tonic and wound balm. The corolla is shaped like a sickle, reflecting in the doctrine of signatures its nature as a carpenter herb. Energetically, it guides our healing path and opens us up to change and transformation. Self-heal mends hearts, protects and prepares the psyche and soul for healing.

Cornflower (*Centaurea cyanus*), also called starthistle or bachelor's buttons, was traditionally worn by men in love. It was thought that if the blue colour of the petals faded quickly, their love was unrequited. In Greek mythology, Cyanus was found dead in a field of cornflowers, and was turned into one by the goddess Chloris. In the language of flowers, the cornflower symbolizes purity, strength and courage. It also has associations with fertility and was said to bring protection and inspiration.

A funerary herb for the ancient Egyptians, it symbolized the cycles of life after death, and was one of the flowers found in the garland in Tutankhamun's tomb. Cornflower continues to hold this frequency of healing and resurrection in more recent years, as, like poppies, they were seen growing from the disturbed soils of World War One battlefields in France.

A visionary plant, it was used as an eye bath to soothe the eyes, but also to increase clairvoyance and connect to the outer edges of our awareness, allowing healing of those parts that are hidden or in our blind spots.

METHOD

1 Place cleaned cornflower flower heads into the alembic pot (alternatively, you can use the saucepan method) and cover completely with water.

2 Leave to sit for an hour to allow the flowers to absorb the moisture.

3 Place the minaret dome onto the pot and connect the condenser.

4 Hermetically seal the still.

5 Fill a bucket with cold water (adding ice if in a warm climate), and connect the condenser with the piping to pump cold water around the coil.

6 Turn on the recirculating pump.

7 Light the flame and place a glass beaker under the condenser pipe to gather the hydrosol.

8 Once no more hydrosol is produced, bottle and store in a cool, dark place.

APPLICATION

Take a few drops on the tongue or add to bath water to call upon the healing wisdom of Chiron.

Uranus

Beyond the physical, earthbound limits of Saturn lies Uranus. Out in the transpersonal domain in the literal heavens, it is also known as 'father sky to Gaia's Earth', 'King of the Titans' and 'father to Saturn'. Its rebellious nature rejects the institutional and cultural structures of Saturn in favour of a higher octave of the individual soul for the benefit of the collective. The glyph for Uranus is the cross of matter presiding over the circle of spirit, flanked by two receptive crescents either side. An alternative glyph is the arrow of action pointing in the direction of the heavens, while the central dot in the circle of spirit represents the inner wisdom of the soul.

Gaia gave birth to Uranus and, in turn, gave birth to their children, which Uranus despised, insisting that they remain underground, hidden in her body. She appealed to Cronos (Saturn), who castrated his father with a sickle. The blood that fell impregnated Gaia, who gave birth to the Furies, the Giants and the Meliai (ash-tree nymphs). The genitals of Uranus fell to the sea, and turned to foam, from which sprang the goddess of love, Aphrodite.

With a highly eccentric orbit that takes approximately 84 years, and spinning sideways on its axis, Uranus was discovered during the Enlightenment in 1781 by Sir William Herschel. It was a time of revolutions, innovations, electricity and scientific endeavour. This is the signature of Uranus: highly unique and a true visionary; independent, liberated and interested in revolutionizing old structures and cultural institutions. Uranus offers a new lens and a new way of being, and governs robotics, AI, technology and futuristic exploits. Uranus is domicile in Aquarius, in detriment in Leo, exalted in Scorpio and in fall in Taurus. With Capricorn, it rules the tenth house of career and ambition. Like Jupiter, it has an association with lightning, which enters into our realms as a flash of inspiration. Uranus transmits new waves of intergalactic information and illuminates our path towards our true essence. The placement of Uranus in a chart can channel an electrical charge or concentration of the vital force in that area.

Uranus, who rules Aquarius in modern astrology, governs electricity in the body and its rhythms, the pulse of the nervous system, the beat of the heart and the rate of flow of the metabolism. Uranus has correspondences to heart attacks, epilepsy, electrical shocks and sudden accidents. Uranus plants are stimulating and sharpen focus and function, and may be blue, which is the colour of the planet.

Coffee (*Coffee arabica*) is an archetypal Uranus plant, stimulating the nervous system and metabolism, increasing blood flow to the brain and activating nonadrenal neurons. Echinacea (*Echinacea purpurea*) is another plant of Uranus, stimulating the immune system. Elecampane (*Inula helenium*) was known as elfwort, and was used to protect against the tricks of mischievous elf folk and enhance psychic visions. It supports Uranus in balancing the rhythms of the nervous, circulatory and digestive systems.

Other stimulants, such as gotu kola, ginkgo, cacao and brahmi are also under the guidance of Uranus. Additional plants with connections and resonances to Uranus include allspice, cacao, chicory, dandelion, kola nut, lady's mantle, mandrake, spikenard, true unicorn root, white pine and wild carrot.

Chicory Root Coffee

Chicory (*Cichorium intybus*) is a bitter digestive, diuretic and tonic, and its magical properties are assistant in redirecting your path, allowing you to see things from an alternative perspective. In the language of flowers, it symbolizes faith and love, particularly that which is unrequited or in vain.

Opening its flowers only briefly, chicory teaches patience – a counter-balance to the sudden nature of Uranus that strikes when least expected. Maidens would place the buds on themselves and, if the flowers opened, they would expect their love to appear. Their signature blue colour honours the sky and the sky god Uranus.

Botanist Carl Linnaeus created the Horologium Florae – a flower clock, whereby the flowers planted would open and close in sequence, telling the time. Versions with chicory place it between 5am and 11am, which chimes with the common rhyme: 'In the mornings, they're blue / By midday, they're through.' Although usually blue, rare white or pink flowers sometimes appear that are thought to have magical powers. Chicory root was thought to be protective and offer invisibility, which may mean that energetically, it assists in removing obstacles.

METHOD

1 Dig up the chicory roots when flowering is complete in autumn. When the Moon is in Aquarius or Uranus is in a favourable position, wash and soak the roots before slicing and chopping them into equal-size pieces, saving a little of the root for the application process (see below).
2 Roast them until they turn a golden brown.
3 Grind them to a fine powder with a few allspice berries in a coffee grinder (to taste) or suitable blender with a grinding capacity.
4 Place in a percolator or a Japanese tea infuser and fill with cold water. Let it sit for 24 hours until the water turns dark for a cold brew.
5 Alternatively, use the ground chicory as you would normal coffee with hot water filtration. Add a few drops of chicory flower essence before drinking.

APPLICATION

Before drinking, burn a little of the root on hot coals and tune in to the energetics of Uranus and the field of potential that lies within it. Ask to channel its creative qualities and to remove obstacles in order to receive new information and insights.

Neptune

The glyph of Neptune is the cross of matter mounted by the crescent of the soul, also interpreted as the trident held by Neptune (or Poseidon in Greek mythology), god of the sea, pointing in the direction of the heavens, symbolizing the cosmic ocean. Neptune represents the great beyond, the subtle realms of the collective unconscious and the illuminated soul. It allows us to see that we are all part of this vast ocean. It is associated with mysticism, spiritual practice and meditative states of bliss and enlightenment. Neptune's orbit takes around 165 years, so its themes are intergenerational, spanning epochs. Alchemically, it is the ethereal solution, a return to the primordial waters of the *prima materia*. It dissolves into chaos, but also has the potential to be the solvent that brings about cohesion and coagulation.

Its influence manifests as highly intuitive, sensitive and psychic or altered states of consciousness. It rules over the domain of our dreams and can, like the tale of the sirens, lure sailors to their deaths, pulling the psyche into a state of *maya* or escapism and becoming detached from reality, and for this reason it is associated with hedonism and drug addiction. In a chart, it has a diffusive quality that can make what it touches elusive and mysterious. Neptune transits give birth to the unborn parts of our psyche floating in Neptune's primordial seas. Our dreams, illusions and fantasies surface and are reflected back to be seen as they truly are; if they are narcissistic delusions to be dissolved and evolved, or ideals to be awakened into the collective.

Neptune can bring great insight, but requires an anchor. Intuition needs to be grounded in reality to integrate the collective and the higher aspects of our soul into our spirit and physical reality. Due to its lack of boundaries, Neptune rules over infectious disease, addiction, mysterious or unexplained illness, poisoning and mental health issues, influencing the fluids of the brain with the Moon and the nerves in the brain with Mercury and Uranus. Neptune is domicile in Pisces, in detriment in Virgo, exalted in Leo and in fall in Aquarius, although some astrologers place exaltation in Cancer and fall in Capricorn. With Pisces, it rules the twelfth house, sometimes referred to as 'the house of undoing' with its focus on transformation through the hidden, secret and intangible; this speaks the diffusive and illusive nature of Neptune.

Plants of Neptune are often sedatives, enhancing sleep and dreams, or narcotics. They sometimes have colours of blue and purple, such as passionflower (*Passiflora incarnata*), which is a nervine and sedative that has the signature of Neptune (traditionally ruled by Venus).

It also supports psychic expansion and connection to spirit. As a dream herb, mugwort (*Artemisia vulgaris*) is an ally of Neptune and assists with accessing lucid dream states that allow for deeper investigation of the liminal and the subconscious. Willow (*Salix alba*) is a plant of Neptune, and helps to dissolve the pains of suffering when one has drifted into a space of wallowing; it gives us the strength to face reality again. Seaweeds such as kelp and bladderwrack, and coastal plants such as sea lavender, sea kale and samphire also hold Neptunian signatures.

Other examples would be psychoactive plants such as opium poppy and cannabis, along with calming plants that relax and induce sleep such as kava kava, blue lotus and bobinsana.

Seaweed Bath

Bladderwrack (*Fucus vesiculosus*) is rich in minerals and nutrients such as iron, zinc, magnesium and potassium. It is well known for its high content of bioavailable iodine, which supports the endocrine system, thyroid function and the metabolism.

It is traditionally used to treat joint pains, gout, tuberculosis and, more recently, eyesight. It is also high in fucoidan, a sulfated polysaccharide that supports a healthy inflammatory response. It expands psychic awareness and assists in connecting to the liminal, dreamy realms of Neptune. Dried bladderwrack and other seaweeds have a folk use of being hung outside the door as a barometer. If it remains dry, then clear, sunny weather is expected, and if it rehydrates, becoming plump and flexible from the moisture in the air, foul weather is predicted. It is also thought to protect and guide those at sea.

Also known as sea herb, sea spirit or sea oak, bladderwrack offers its magic when cast into the sea, with the intention of summoning the spirits within – the undines, mermaids and other water beings – for guardianship. In Roman mythology, sea goddess Salacia was crowned with seaweed, while Thalassa, the personification of the sea in Greek mythology, was depicted dressed in seaweed.

METHOD

1 When by the sea, ideally when the Moon is full in Pisces, or when Neptune is transiting your chart, gather bladderwrack, kelp and other fresh seaweed. Ensure that the area of sea you are collecting from shows no signs of pollution and is away from heavy industry. Fill a bottle with sea water.

2 Rinse the plants very gently in filtered water. You want to remove any sand or contaminants, but retain the benefits of the sea water and the mucilaginous properties of the seaweed.

3 Run a bath and add the seawater to the bath water. Add the seaweed, enter the bath and soak.

4 Rub the seaweed over your skin and hair, or use the seaweed as a poultice by wrapping it over a particular area of your body. High in collagen, it will leave skin and hair silky.

5 Dive into this sensory experience and allow the bladderwrack to connect you to the sea itself, asking it to reveal something to you.

APPLICATION

Apply using the methods above to call upon Neptune for insight and to journey to the imaginary realms.

Caution: For external use only.

Pluto

Pluto is a dwarf planet in the Kuiper belt, discovered in 1930, at what became a profoundly destructive and transformative time of global crisis – the creation of the atomic bomb (plutonium), and the heralding of World War II. This was around the time of the Great Depression and dictatorial rule throughout Europe. Pluto is Greek Hades, Chthonic god and lord of the underworld, and is connected to the subconscious mind and the collective unconscious. Pluto is associated with chaos and annihilation, but this destructive force, as we see in the alchemical process, is transformational. It is concerned with personal and transpersonal power. Pluto's glyph places soul and spirit above matter, and suggests a receptivity to the underworld, with the superconscious sitting above the physical world. Pluto's cycle is 248 years, and it spends between 12 and 30 years in each sign.

As we transcend from the boundary condition of Saturn and through the radical lens of Uranus, swimming in the illuminated amniotic waters of Neptune, Pluto demands a rebirthing. It assists Saturn in the calcination process as a powerful, devouring and destructive force. Our passions, instincts and creativity are offered up as fuel to the flame. It demands death to the old in order to build the new, and as we float into the hypnotic waters of Neptune, we soothe the trauma of our death and are reborn through the new *vesica piscis* of Uranus and Saturn, which assists us in rebuilding a brave new world. Pluto transits are generational and can herald upheaval, war and revolution. Together, Uranus, Neptune and Pluto form another higher-dimensional union of soul, spirit and matter respectively. Pluto is domicile in Scorpio, in detriment in Taurus, exalted in Aries and in fall in Libra, although some astrologers place exaltation in Leo and fall in Cancer. With Scorpio, it rules the eighth house of sex, death and rebirth.

Pluto's influence in a chart or through a transit asks us where some part of us needs to be let go. It requires that we journey into the underworld to face our inner demons and slay the dragon. Pluto's transits reflects our internal and external power dynamics, and reveals what treasure lies beneath our conscious awareness, as we must journey deep below the surface of our reality to discover the precious metals of the earth. As with any alchemical preparation, the plant must die to release its soul for transformation, as death is the begetter of life.

Pluto corresponds to the lower digestive and genito-urinary tracts in the body, and diseases linked to radiation, pandemics and parasites. Pluto plants might smell, exist underground, be carnivorous and have dark purple or black mottled flesh. The mandrake (*Mandragora officinarum*) is a potent plant used in magic and witchcraft, containing hallucinogenic and narcotic alkaloids. Pomegranate (*Punica granatum*) is the fruit of the underworld that Persephone ate from, binding her to Hades (Pluto) for six months of the year; a month for every seed she swallowed.

All mushrooms, as consumers of that which rots and dies, transformers and death-workers of the world beneath us, bear the Pluto signature of death and regeneration. Many are deadly poisonous with names such as ghost pipe and death cap. They are beacons of a hidden, secret underworld. Some fungi are able to decompose radioactive material, which is an aspect of Pluto.

Poisonous plants that bring us closer to death are also Plutonic, such as deadly nightshade (*Atropa belladonna*), poison hemlock (*Conium maculatum*), and monkshood (*Aconitum napellus*). Other plants associated with Pluto include astragalus, black cohosh, dragon's blood, ginseng, ground ivy, turkey tail and yew.

Ground Ivy and Turkey Tail Digestif

Ground ivy (*Glechoma hederacea*) was also called alehoof, which comes from its use by the Anglo-Saxons to flavour and clarify beer before the use of hops. Similarly, it works to clarify brain fog, and was used to treat colds, sore throats, sinusitis, headaches and hay fever.

It is a creeping plant and considered invasive in its growth, spreading across the ground and seeking out and covering shaded areas. Energetically, it clears the psychic channels and has strong associations with witchcraft, where it is used as a herb of protection against curses and spells. It is grounding and draws excess mucus and water into the earth element. It was said that by wearing ground ivy, you would be able to see who in your village was a witch, and that similarly, it would show you the parts that people keep secret. In the language of flowers, it symbolizes assertiveness and divination.

Turkey tail (*Trametes versicolor*) grows on dead and dying wood, bearing the transformational signature of Pluto, and shares a similar fan-shaped structure as the leaves of ground ivy. In combination, this remedy serves to alleviate stagnation and rigid patterns of earth by purifying the blood, stimulating the metabolism and supporting digestion through the breaking down of toxins and their elimination. It is a good immune tonic and has high concentrations of polysaccharide K, used in some treatments for cancer and chronic fatigue syndrome.

METHOD

1 Gather turkey tail mushrooms and ground ivy leaves on Saturn's day (Saturday).
2 Brush the mushrooms clean of debris. Wash the ground ivy leaves.
3 Make a decoction of your turkey tails. Many beneficial compounds are water-soluble, so this is ideally done twice to ensure full extraction. A slow cooker is ideal for this: cover the turkey tails in water and set to low overnight, then in the morning, strain the liquid and set aside. Add more water and repeat.
4 Once done, combine the two liquids and steep the ground ivy leaves.
5 Optionally, add a blend of dried bitter earth herbs to taste, such as yellow dock, chaparral or walnut leaves. Add spices (if desired), such as cardamom and orange peel.
6 Combine all the ingredients into a bottle and top up with brandy or vodka. Put in a cool, dark place and agitate regularly for three weeks, then strain.

APPLICATION

Drink in moderation as an aperitif or digestif. It may be diluted with tonic or soda water. If you prefer, dilute 1 tablespoon in warm water.

The Zodiac

Zodiac is derived from the Greek *zodiakos*, meaning 'circle of animals'. Astrology is a dynamic system of elements. Fire and air signs are considered to be active, while earth and water signs are passive, which really means receptive. The zodiac signs are divided into the four elements, so that there are three signs within each element. Within these three expressions of an element, there are three further qualities called modes. These are cardinal, mutable and fixed, which relate to the *tria prima* of sulphur, mercury and salt. Each element has a threefold form, which progresses from the gross to the subtle as we move through the houses of the chart and the astrological seasons of the year.

Water gives a clear visual example of how one element can be expressed in multiple ways: fixed water is ice, mutable water is liquid, and cardinal water is steam, rising from the physical to the spiritual. Cardinal energy initiates the season and is quick, active and inspirational. In the body, this can mean acute and fleeting conditions that are aggressive but short-lived. Mutable energy transitions from one season to the next and is changeable, fluctuating and communicates the ideas of the other modes out into the world. In the body, these qualities can manifest as conditions that are volatile, sporadic and recurring. Fixed energy embodies the cardinal energy and slows it down, fixing it into reality,

and this is expressed at the peak moment of a season. Fixed conditions might be chronic or hereditary. Each sign has its archetype and its opposite, with which they share the same modality – for example, both Aries and Libra are cardinal signs. So to understand the signs fully, we must look for context to the opposite, as they share a special resonance and each is reflected in the other. It is a mirror and a dance. This is known as polarity. It could be seen that there are fundamentally six signs with dual expressions, with polarities in the body and systems that they govern. While they teach each other about their emotional, mental and psycho-spiritual journey, in medical astrology, the organs ruled by the opposite sign may reveal information about an illness of the other.

There are twelve houses in a chart, created by spinning the Earth on its axis during one day. Each of the twelve houses describes an aspect of life and the journey we make from birth, through adolescence, adulthood and finally old age and death. The houses follow the astrological year, so the first house is under the dominion of the sign of Aries, and the twelfth house under the dominion of Pisces. A chart can be cast for any moment in time, and is used in medical astrology to identify the onset of disease, for timings of surgery and for remedy-taking.

A natal chart is a snapshot of the cosmic wheel at the moment of birth when we take our first breath, and it presents a crystalline matrix of our astral structure and the flow of energy. This is defined by the exact moment of birth by time, date and geographical location. This is as if the central spoke of the wheel is the crown of your head, and it shows in which section of the wheel the Sun (sun or star sign, the core principles of the self), the Moon (moon sign, the inward expression of the self) and the planets are positioned at that moment. It also shows which planet is rising (the rising sign, also called the ascendant, is how we project ourselves externally and how we are perceived by others) on the horizon. From a physiological perspective, the chart is a guide towards constitutional elemental dynamics.

MODALITIES

- Earth signs: Taurus (fixed), Virgo (mutable), Capricorn (cardinal)
- Water signs: Cancer (cardinal), Scorpio (fixed), Pisces (mutable)
- Air signs: Gemini (mutable), Libra (cardinal), Aquarius (fixed)
- Fire signs: Aries (cardinal), Leo (fixed), Sagittarius (mutable)

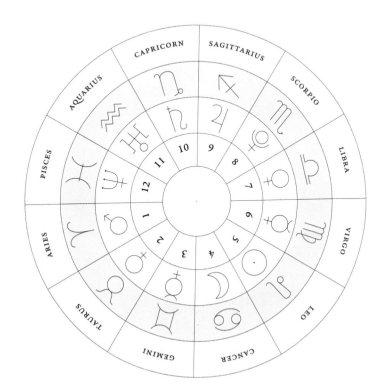

HOUSE QUALITIES

INNER WORLD
1. Self and personality
2. Value and resources
3. Communication and travel
4. Home and family
5. Creativity and pleasure
6. Health and service

OUTER WORLD
7. Love and relationships
8. Sex, death and rebirth
9. Philosophy and higher learning
10. Career and status
11. Community
12. Sacrifice and secrets

Popular culture and horoscopes have placed considerable emphasis on the position of the Sun in a chart. However, when the whole chart is viewed, someone who has the sun sign of Cancer, ruled by the water element, might have a stellium of five planets in a fire sign in one of their houses, dramatically altering their constitutional archetype.

The communication between the planetary bodies and the chart creates the arising of potential states that can have an impact on the individual. The planets passing through the chart act as triggers, catalysing certain conditions. The frequency of these transits depends on the length of the orbit of a planet and how and when it will interact with a chart. We have a monthly lunar transit and an annual solar transit – our birthday. Transiting Mars will heat up and activate where it passes, while Saturn will cool down and constrict. The orbital periods increase the further away the planets are in the solar system. Where the planet is positioned in a chart will depend on the quality and intensity of its impact. A retrograde phase is when a planet pauses in its orbit and gives the illusion of going backwards in the sky. Energetic influence weakens and becomes inward and reflective, and retrograde seasons are a time for stillness and reflection.

Working with the planetary transits can transform our alchemical process. Mars on our Sun or ascendant gives us the drive we need to complete an action, while the outer planets offer a more layered, existential unfolding to occur. Transits highlight the areas in our lives where our growth or evolution is compromised.

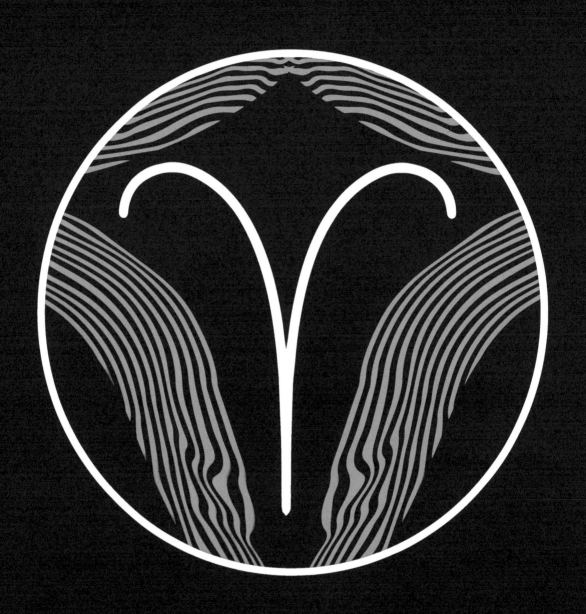

Aries

(MARCH 21–APRIL 19)

In the Northern Hemisphere, the zodiac begins at the spring equinox, when days and night are equal in length. It is a time of renewed energy, anticipation and inspiration; a time to take action and prepare for the year ahead, sharpening arrows and spears for hunting. Aries watches over the first house on the chart, which represents the vital force that flows through the self – the personality, the ego, personal will and power. The glyph for Aries is the horns of the ram, which drive forwards with force and determination. Aries is ruled by Roman Mars (Ares is the Greek god of war, equivalent to Mars). Its metal is iron, and it is active, hot and dry: fire. It is a cardinal sign, corresponding to the initial alchemical process of calcination, the first act of purification. Its esoteric ruler is Mercury, which encourages right communication of these active forces. Aries governs the head, eyes and upper jaw, and can be subject to excess heat or dryness, headaches, sinus issues and high blood pressure. Its polarity is Libra; while Aries holds a mirror to the self, Libra holds the mirror towards others. In their own ways, they both take their lead. The highly energetic and driven qualities of Aries can lead to frustration and stagnation if not channelled appropriately. Impatiens flower essence and decongestant herbs are allies in remedying these respectively.

Aries plants correspond to the Sun and Mars, which stimulate and drive the energies of the body, fighting infection with morphology of thorns, serrated leaves, fast growth patterns and pioneer plants that thrive in hostile places, such as rosebay willowherb (*Chamaenerion angustifolium*), the first plant to grow after a fire. Nettle (*Urtica dioica*) is a prominent Aries plant with these signatures. Aries tendencies are remedied by the cooling waters of lunar plants, particularly their action on the fluids of the brain.

Supportive plants like basil (*Ocimum basilicum*) are a good plant ally for Aries. Ruled by Mars, it is an anti-inflammatory and antispasmodic that tonifies the blood, calms the nervous system and relieves sinus congestion. The essential oil has a dual action in that it is at once grounding and calming to the mind while also uplifting and aiding concentration. Wild garlic (*Allium ursinum*), also called ramsons, has the pungent signature of Mars and assists Aries as a blood tonic, purifying the blood, improving circulation, helping lower blood pressure, and reducing cholesterol in the blood. It has long been used in folk remedies to ward off colds and flu. To wood betony (*Betonica officinalis*) Culpeper corresponds Jupiter in Aries, and it is used for headaches, particularly those originating from tension or digestive issues. It was held in such high esteem that the proverb goes, 'Sell your coat and buy betony.'

Other plants with correspondences to Aries include bilberry, cinnamon, cowslip, dragon's blood, frankincense, ginger, holly, horseradish, pepper, rosemary, sweet marjoram, thistle and yarrow.

Bilberry Cordial

Bilberry (*Vaccinium myrtillus*) is rich in anthocyanins, supporting eyesight by strengthening the blood vessels of the eyes.

According to Greek mythology, bilberries were created when Hermes turned the body of his son Myrtillus into a shrub after he was murdered and cast into the sea for sabotaging the chariot of King Oenomaus in the hopes of a night with his daughter, Hippodamia.

The antioxidant berries are a worthy blood tonic, strengthening the veins and capillaries. Energetically, bilberry can assist in strengthening our visionary channels, helping to extend the horizons of Aries to see beyond the now. In the language of flowers, it is linked to prayer and connection to the sacred.

METHOD

1 Cover your bilberries with water and simmer gently until the flesh dissolves.
2 Strain through muslin or a jelly bag and return the strained liquid to the pan.
3 Add raw sugar at a ratio of 1:3 sugar to liquid.
4 Heat and stir until the sugar has dissolved, then pour into sterilized bottles or jars.

APPLICATION

Take 1 teaspoon neat – or dilute in warm water and drink as a tonic – as required. When you take it, close your eyes and concentrate on your inner vision, allowing any insight and images to arise.

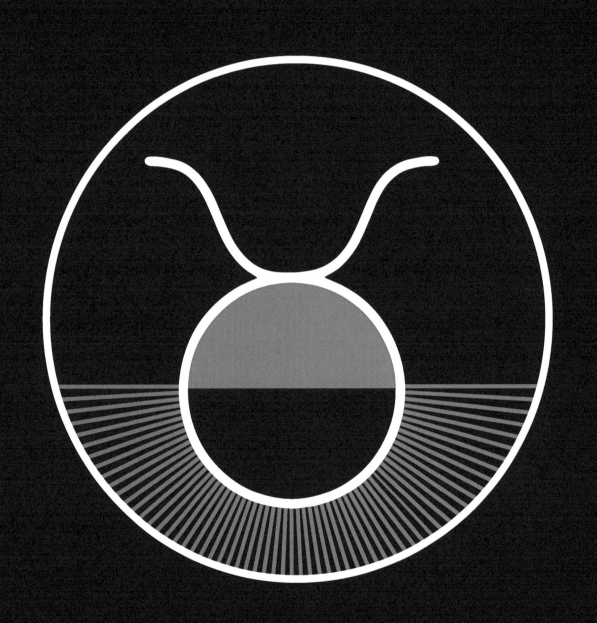

Taurus

After the initiating energetic force of Aries season, Taurus season is a time for communing with the land now that the frost has thawed. It is time to tend to the soil, sow seeds and make preparations for a stable future. It is innately practical, connecting to the material pleasures and senses and delighting in nature and food. This marks the peak of spring, when this season is in its most fixed form and reflects a time of manifestation into the physical. The glyph for Taurus is a bull, symbolizing fertility and agriculture, and also the goddess through its connection to the Moon, seen in its crescent horns and its planetary ruler of Venus. The esoteric ruler is Vulcan, a hypothetical planet named after the god of fire, volcanos and metal work. It illuminates the free flow of will and power for the evolved consciousness of Taurus to see actions through to completion. As a fixed earth sign, it is associated with the process of congelation, of grounding and consolidating to allow for fertility and growth. Copper is its metal, reflecting its ability to ground and conduct information into the earth. Taurus is moist and warm, a receptive sign. It rules the second house: our material world and immediate physical environment. While Taurus explores through the material and tangible, it also learns through its opposite sign, Scorpio, which experiences through the emotional and intangible.

Taurus rules the lower jaw, neck, larynx, throat, vocal cords and ears. The correspondence to sensual pleasures and fixed mid-season modality can cause excess body weight and a refusal to flow, causing stagnation in the energetics and physiology. Oak flower essence supports Taurus when overburdened with the weight of responsibility, and hornbeam helps to lift us out of states of inertia and reluctance. Taurus plants are the plants of Venus. Rose (*Rosa spp.*) is an archetypal plant of Taurus, offering support in developing the strength and grace of the voice. Taurus plants can also be deep-rooted, low-lying and nutrient-dense. They can be fixed earth and astringent. Stagnation, the build up of toxins, and other such complaints of Taurus

benefit from lymphatic cleansing herbs like cleavers (*Galium aparine*) and gentle warming stimulants like sage (*Salvia officinalis*), which creates movement and supports digestive function.

Supportive plants like burdock (*Arctium lappa*) help Taureans to clear conditions of excess earth when the body becomes slow and sluggish, encouraging the body to release toxins. Common mallow (*Malva sylvestris*) is a prolific mucilaginous herb that soothes the throat and purifies the blood. The leaves can be eaten like spinach or in place of vine leaves. The seeds can be toasted and the pink flowers can be added to salads or pickled. Elder (*Sambucus nigra*) supports the immune system, while thyme (*Thymus vulgaris*) is a suitable plant ally, ruled by Mercury and Venus. It is an antiseptic and antifungal, and its antispasmodic properties have long been called upon as a traditional remedy for sore throats, coughs, chest infections and ear congestion. It also improves digestion and relieves gas and parasites. An oil made from mullein (*Verbascum thapus*) can be used to heal and maintain the ears.

Other Taurus plants include chicory, coltsfoot, daisy, fern, fig, honeysuckle, lady's mantle, linden, lovage, mint, myrtle, oak, olive, rosemary and tansy.

Elderflower and
Thyme Honey

Elder (*Sambucus nigra*) is an earth element plant ruled by Venus, and is a blood purifier that assists in the stagnation or excess earth that Taureans are prone to. It has antibacterial and antiviral properties, making it a traditional cold and flu remedy.

Elder integrates the air element into the earth through water. Energetically, elder has potent magical correspondences and protective energy. It is associated with death and rebirth – the end of one cycle and the beginning of the next. Guarded by the Elder Mother, permission must be asked of her before harvesting, and it was said that to cut an elder tree without the right permissions would cause death to fall on the perpetrator within three days. According to folklore, when elder burns, it is said to scream. It has a relationship with music, and Pliny the Elder called it the pipe tree due to its hollow stems, which were used to make whistles, trumpets and bagpipes. In the language of flowers, it stands for compassion.

Thyme (*Thymus vulgaris*) is antibacterial and antimicrobial, purifying the system against invasion, and was burnt in temples for purification and fortitude. Pliny the Elder said that when thyme is burned, it 'puts to flight all venomous creatures'. In the Middle Ages, it was placed under pillows to ward off nightmares and evil thoughts. It was embroidered on the garments of Roman generals and given to the crusaders before battle. Other species of thyme, including *Thymus praecox*, could be used in the making of this remedy. In the language of flowers, thyme symbolizes courage, strength and sacrifice.

METHOD
1 Pick your elder and thyme flowers. You may use thyme leaves if not in flower, or a combination of leaves and flowers.
2 Remove the stalks and submerge the flower heads into a pot of raw local honey.
3 Seal and allow to infuse for a week, or to taste, before straining.

APPLICATION
Take 1 teaspoon directly or dissolved in warm water as a tonic to relieve sore throats. You may also mix the honey with marshmallow root powder to create pastilles (see page 139).
Caution: The leaves, bark and raw berries of elder are toxic.

Gemini

As a mutable sign, Gemini transitions from spring to summer. After the initiatory preparations of Aries and Taurus, this is a time of activity and growth within the community through communication – the energetics of the third house. It is the thinking element of air, hot, moist and active. Gemini season is time to receive information from the environment, to send messages to other tribes and distant relatives for insight, and to reach out beyond the immediate environment to network and process new information. This is expressed in Gemini's correspondence to pairs in the body – hands, lungs, shoulders and arms, and the nervous system. Its metal is mercury or quicksilver, which is fluid and mobile, and has a fast molecular motion. Gemini, too, with its agile mind, is quick to change state. Gemini resonates with the alchemical process of fixation, the act of stabilizing volatile components through the union of the higher and lower mind, clear communication and right timing. Like its ruler Mercury, it influences speech and hearing.

Gemini's glyph here shows the duality of the pair, separate yet ultimately united as one. Gemini plants are mercurial plants that balance the nervous system, and their morphology often corresponds to signatures of nerve fibres, neurons or bronchioles. The esoteric ruler of Gemini is Venus, stablising the flight of the mind through love and the intelligence of the heart. While Geminis are focused on the present, curious and eager to question and investigate their immediate environment, their polarity, Sagittarius, applies the same agility of mind but with a passion for going beyond the horizon, to see the bigger picture. The remedy plants for Gemini conditions of anxiety, hypertension, nervous exhaustion and insomnia are met with nutritive plants with a downwards energy. Cerato essence assists in trusting inner guidance over external influence.

Supportive plants like gotu kola (*Centella asiatica*) are a good ally for Gemini. Ruled by Mercury and Uranus, it has a dual influence on the nerves and brain. A relaxant and mild sedative, gotu kola relieves and restores the nervous system, while at the same time enhancing mental function and memory recall. Meadowsweet (*Filipendula ulmaria*) is a herb of Gemini, containing salicylic acid for pain relief, and aiding rheumatism and arthritis in the joints. Restorative nutritive plants, like milky oats (*Avena sativa*) and soporific passionflower (*Passiflora incarnata*), and mercurial nervine herbs like lavender (*Lavandula angustifolia*) and skullcap (*Scutellaria lateriflora*) calm the nervous system.

Other Gemini plants include bergamot, caraway, clove, dill, Douglas fir, gorse, honeysuckle, mastic, mint, mugwort, mulberry, mullein, oregano, parsley, thyme, vervain and walnut.

Meadowsweet and Honeysuckle Mead

Meadowsweet (*Filipendula ulmaria*, opposite) shares similar properties as an anti-inflammatory and pain reliever to those of willow (*Salix alba*). They both have high concentrations of salicylic acid (the phenolic glycoside from which aspirin was first synthesized).

Like willow, meadowsweet is used to treat arthritis and areas where the spaces in between joints are painful. It has a long history of being used to treat the lungs and airways, respiratory conditions, coughs and colds due to its anti-inflammatory and expectorant properties. It forms part of a tryptic of three herbs held sacred by the Druids, the other two being vervain (*Verbena officinalis*) and water mint (*Mentha aquatica*). It has been used for all manner of digestive complaints, including digestive headaches and heartburn, calming and balancing the pH of the stomach. It has also been used to ease coughs and colds. Archaeological evidence suggests it has been used to flavour beer with its delicate bitter almond notes since around 3000 BC. Known as 'Queen of the Meadows', energetically, it is used in love magic, and it encourages self-love.

Honeysuckle (*Lonicera periclumenum*) is a calming nervine and works to clear excess heat from the blood, cool inflammation and pull out heat caused by stress and anger. As a respiratory aid, it is soothing to the mucous membranes and can be used as a cough remedy. Energetically, it is protective and attracts prosperity. It is thought to be auspicious and to bring luck when growing around a home. In the language of flowers, it represents love, fidelity and devotion.

METHOD

1 These flowers can be picked in June, ideally when the Moon is also in Gemini.
2 On a full moon, make an infusion of the flowers using hot filtered water at a ratio of 5:1 flowers to water. Allow to steep for 15 minutes.
3 Transfer into a sterilized fermentation bucket, and add honey to the infusion at a ratio of 4:1 honey to liquid, stirring vigorously – this is not just to dissolve the honey, but also to activate the natural yeast in the flowers, which catalyses the fermentation process. This method requires favourable conditions, so you may wish to add brewer's yeast to safeguard the process.
4 Cover with a muslin cloth. Keep in a warm place or at room temperature, away from direct sunlight, such as in a cupboard.
5 Stir daily and check the quality of your mead for changes in odour and any signs of spoiling. It should be bubbling well and the temperature, measured with a thermometer, should be stable at around 15–20°C during the primary fermentation.
6 On the new moon, pass the mead through a siphon to remove sediment, and transfer it into a sterilized demijohn fitted with a bung and airlock. After the full lunation is complete on the full moon, it should be ready, but taste for acidity and check for signs of mould – it should smell sweet and yeasty.

APPLICATION

Drink in moderation to calm the nerves and support the lungs.
Caution: Do not use if you have an allergy to salicylates. Honeysuckle leaves and berries are toxic.

Cancer

(JUNE 21–JULY 22)

After the planning and preparatory work of the spring, Cancer season is a time to return to the fourth house – the home. As a cardinal sign it welcomes in a new season and energetic matrix with new ways of being that are focused on the sensual, feeling and emotional welfare of the individual within the family network. The thinking, air quality of Gemini now grounds into the emotional body for a time of integration and reflection through the water element. Emotions are heightened and the lunar archetype of the mother is invoked. Its metal is silver, and Cancer is cold, moist and receptive. It corresponds to dissolution and solution in alchemy, through the merging of the conscious and unconscious emotions to be released. Its glyph of the crab symbolizes protection, and the cardinal quality of the defensive pincers contrast to the sensitive body within. In mythology, the crab is a symbol of Hera's fierce protection of her brood.

Cancer governs the breasts, ribcage, stomach, mucous membranes and womb. If imbalanced, it can cause boundary issues within the tissues and within the emotional body, particularly in sync with the waxing and waning of the Moon. Cancer plants are ruled by the Moon and will often be found close to water. The esoteric ruler is Neptune, evolving from lunar emanations of ancestry, memory and emotions into the realms of imagination in order to move beyond the self, into the transpersonal. Cancer's opposite sign, Capricorn, communicates with the outer world rather than Cancer's inner nature. On the spectrum of agency, Cancer is dependent whereas Capricorn is independent. Plants to remedy afflictions of Cancer are hot and dry to balance its cold and moist nature; they are mercurial to calm the nervous system and liver, digestive tonics and diuretics to address excess fluids; or Saturnian and earth element plants to give structure and create boundaries. Cancerians benefit from honeysuckle flower essence when they become too attached to the emotions of the past, red chestnut when they become too fearful and over-protective of their loved ones, and cleavers when they become too clingy in relationships.

Supportive plants include lady's mantle (*Alchemilla vulgaris*), which tonifies the waters in the body. Traditionally used to treat the womb and female reproductive system, it also acts on all fluids in the body, including digestive fluids and lymph. The flower essence supports healthy boundaries through the electromagnetic field, protects the heart and encourages connection to the sacred feminine. Common chamomile (*Chamaemelum nobile*) and pineappleweed or wild chamomile (*Matricaria discoidea*) are supportive plants for Cancerians, as they soothe the stomach and relieve undigested emotions, creating the security to feel held in the process. Mugwort (*Artemisia vulgaris*) with its lunar influence and guidance from the goddess Artemis, helps Cancerians in their flow and can be dried and bundled into a smokestick (see page 75) to be burnt for protective purposes.

Other plants that resonate with Cancer include agrimony, angelica, caraway, catnip, daisy, jasmine, lemon balm, lettuce, mallow, melissa, red clover, rosemary, sandalwood, sweet violet and willow.

Sweet Violet
and Pineappleweed
Pastilles

Sweet violet (*Viola odorata*, opposite) is a cooling, moistening herb, acting as a demulcent and expectorant, clearing mucus and also acting as a calming nervine to soothe Cancerians when they feel overwhelmed. Its relative heartsease (*Viola tricolor*) shares the same qualities.

Sweet violet is said to comfort and strengthen the heart, heal deep trauma and soothe the emotional body. It is used in modern herbal medicine to treat stomach and breast cancer. Its heart-shaped leaves are an indicator for its use as a cardiac tonic. Sacred to Dionysus, violets were added to wine and worn as amulets by the Greeks and Romans to prevent hangovers, aid sleep and help them make merry. Amethyst was used in a similar way, and may be added to remedies to enhance this influence. Energetically, violets bring peace and cool heat or anger in the emotional body. Their sweet, alluring scent links them to Aphrodite, Venus and love.

Pineappleweed or wild chamomile (*Matricaria discoidea*) is one of the most aromatic wild varieties – crush the flowering tops of this plant and you are met with the smell of fresh pineapples, hence its name. It is also prolific, found on the edges of fields and pushing through the cracks in urban pavements. Testament to this, in the language of the flowers it means 'strength through adversity', due to the folklore belief that the more trodden it is, the more it grows. Pineappleweed is a calming digestive herb to settle upset stomachs and a relaxing nervine that calms the emotional waters of the body.

METHOD

1 Gather violet flowers and pineappleweed buds on Monday (the Moon's day).
2 Pick the petals from the flowers, along with any leaves. Wash and place in a glass jar with an equal amount of boiling water, and leave to steep overnight in the moonlight, with a crystal of amethyst if you wish.
3 Taking 1 teaspoon of the liquid at a time, blend slowly with raw local honey and marshmallow root until it forms a paste.
4 Roll the paste into balls and leave to airdry.

APPLICATION

Store in an airtight container and suck as lozenges to calm a nervous stomach and soothe your inner waters.

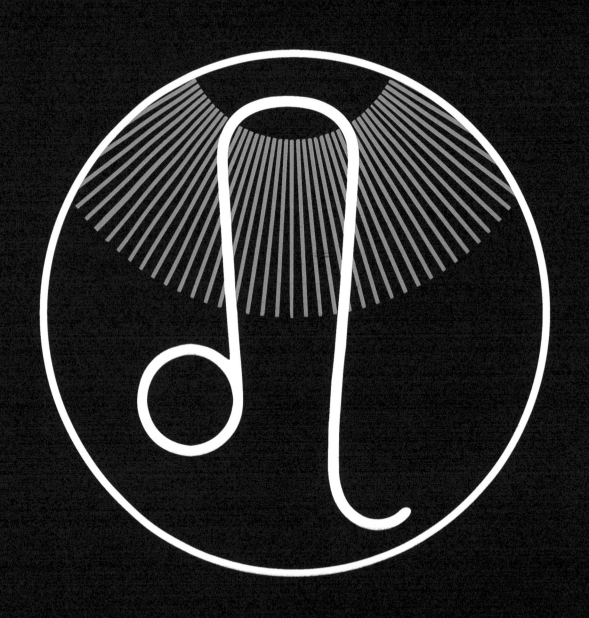

Leo

(JULY 23–AUGUST 22)

At the peak of summer, Leo season comes at a time of celebration and feasting. It rules the fifth house of creative expression and play. This is a time for the individual to emerge from the shell of the crab, and to leave the cocoon of the home and come out into the light to cultivate the self. Ruled by the Sun in both exoteric and esoteric astrology, its metal is gold and it is hot and dry, active and a fixed sign in the middle of the year. Leo's alchemical act is digestion, where it must channel the egoic, creative energies and playful passions into the inner chambers of the higher intelligence of the heart, and from there excite the flames of transformation. This is the fixed fire that follows from the initial spark of Aries and precedes the wisdom of the fire of Sagittarius. The journey of Leo is to transcend the self and master the ego. Through its opposite sign, Aquarius, it experiences the journey from self-expression to collective-expression. The glyph of the lion's mane corresponds to regality, courage, leadership and strength, and asks for the cultivation of inner rather than outer strength.

Leo governs the heart and solar plexus, along with the spine, spinal cord and upper back. The intense excess heat and outwards force of Leo can cause circulatory issues and muscular strain. Leo plants are Sun plants, particularly heart and circulatory tonics such as hawthorn, bay and calming chamomile. Vervain flower essence can assist when Leo energy pushes too hard, and heather when the self suffocates the experience. Plant signatures include bright, disc-shaped, heliotropic flowers that display a rhythm or heartbeat in their growth patterns.

Motherwort (*Leonurus cardiaca*) is a key remedy for Leo and the heart, which is reflected in its botanical name. It supports and strengthens the heart both physiologically and energetically, relieving stress and tension while bestowing a lion's courage. It acts on the rhythms of the cardiovascular system and remedies anxiety and hypertension. Hawthorn (*Crataegus monogyna*) is the primary heart tonic, improving blood flow and nourishing the heart, while cooling Leo excitations, grounding excess energy and acting as a useful digestive aid for indulgent Leos. Borage (*Borago officinalis*) is associated with Leo as it is used as an essence to give courage. Wild cherry (*Prunus avium*) is an astringent, diuretic and tonic that can hold Leo. Nostradamus made an alchemical preparation from cherries that he called 'Clarified Ruby Jelly', which he claimed enhanced prophetic powers and was so potent and refined that it should only be served to noble folk and royalty.

Other Leo plants include angelica, bay, calendula, chamomile, eyebright, frankincense, gorse, heliotrope, lavender, marigold, mistletoe, pineappleweed, rosemary, saffron, St John's wort and walnut.

Hawthorn and Borage Elixir

Known as 'Queen of the May' or the 'Fairy Tree', hawthorn (*Crataegus monogyna*, opposite) is a strong ally for protecting the heart and cardiovascular system, and is a circulatory adaptogen and antioxidant for regulating blood pressure and cholesterol. Borage (*Borago officinalis*) is known as a herb of gladness.

The tree of Beltane, hawthorn is also associated with sexuality, fertility and faery folk. Together with oak and ash, it forms the tryptic of sacred trees in the Celtic tradition. It strengthens the heart and offers protection and cleansing, releasing blocked energy to prepare for spiritual growth. In the language of flowers, it is symbolic of chastity, duality and the union of opposites.

Hawthorn is a profound restorative heart tonic, both in its energetic and biochemical properties. Due to polyphenols and triterpenes, it is able to cool and heat simultaneously, regulating fire in the body and the cardiovascular system. It is high in antioxidants to alleviate damage from free radicals, toning and strengthening the heart and improving cardiovascular tone, vessels and capillary walls. As a diuretic, it cleans the blood through the lymph. Energetically, it heals heartache, grief and sadness.

Pliny the Elder believed that borage was the 'Nepenthe' in Homer's *Odyssey*, causing forgetfulness of worries. The Greeks and Romans regarded borage as the giver of joy and courage. In John Gerard's *Herball*, he says of the plant: 'I, borage bring always courage.'

METHOD

1 Follow the instructions for The Energetic Method on p181 to make a vibrational essence from borage flowers, using brandy or vodka when the Sun is at its zenith at the time of Leo. In spring, cover fresh hawthorn blossoms with brandy, seal the bottle and store in a cool, dark place for 40 days. Shake daily to ensure the liquid fully covers the plant matter.
2 Filter, bottle and store in a cool, dark place.
3 In autumn, add whole hawthorn berries and top up the liquid if required. Leave to tincture for 3 lunar cycles, shaking now and then.
4 Strain and bottle. Add 14 drops of the borage essence to the tincture.

APPLICATION

Hawthorn is slow but deep acting, and so should be taken for a minimum of 3 months, 1 teaspoon a day. Take to alleviate matters of the heart and to give courage and strength.
Caution: Use borage as flower essence only, not for internal use. Remove all green parts, as these contain toxic pyrrolizidine alkaloids.

Virgo

(AUGUST 23–SEPTEMBER 22)

Virgo transitions from summer into autumn, signalling a more reflective time. At the time of the harvest, it is necessary to analyse and plan, mirroring the spring planning of Gemini, as both signs are ruled by Mercury. Where Gemini sees the connections on the surface, Virgo goes deeper and is more detail-orientated, which is necessary in order to calculate supplies accurately and ensure survival through the winter. Virgo is the symbol of the virgin, sometimes depicted holding a sheaf of wheat in correspondence with the grain goddess Demeter. It also corresponds with the myth of Persephone: the descent of the Earth goddess into the underworld and the heralding of a period of darkness, introspection and self-reflection. Its metal is mercury, or quicksilver, reflecting its ability to move quickly through information and process details. It is cold and dry, earth, receptive and mutable. Virgo's alchemical process is distillation, the act of purification through discerning rectification and refinement of the self. A symbol of purity, Virgo moves beyond the egoic self towards a purified expression and one that can be of service to others. Virgo's glyph demonstrates the virgin or maiden turning inward. We can see this mirrored in Scorpio, where the tail turns outwards.

Virgo marks the transition between the two hemispheres of the chart and the movement beyond the evolutionary journey so far, which has been one *of self* – individual consciousness – and into the houses of *the other* – collective consciousness. Virgo's esoteric ruler is the Moon, which evolves the analytical mind of the Virgo into an intuitive one. The sixth house regards health, work and daily life. It is how we digest our experiences and the ways in which we show up for ourselves and manage our expectations of others. Virgo benefits from elm essence when they become over-*elmed* through service, while self-heal essence allows integration of inner wisdom and promotes self-healing. Agrimony essence helps Virgos to release nervous tension when they've taken too much on and are unable to admit it. Beech essence is used for when Virgos

become too judgemental of others, and pine essence is used for feelings of self-criticism and failure.

Virgo governs the small intestines, pancreas and liver (with Sagittarius). Imbalances can lead to nervous and digestive complaints. Although an earth sign, it has a strong relationship to the air element with Mercury as its ruler. It grounds and integrates information into systems, structures and processes. Mercurial plants are Virgo plants, and they are cooling and drying bitters, nervines, relaxants and calmatives, such as fennel (*Foeniculum vulgare*), lemon balm (*Melissa officinalis*) and lavender (*Lavandula angustifolia*).

Supportive plants include parsley (*Petroselinum crispum*), a plant of Mercury that assists Virgo in its quest for purification. By purifying the blood through its action on the liver, and by binding to heavy metals for elimination, it dispels digestive gas and calms the bowels. Wild angelica (*Angelica sylvestris*) assists Virgo in digestion as a stimulating bitter tonic, and is an ally for purification, both physically and energetically.

Other Virgo plants include calamus, chicory, fennel, ginseng, lemon verbena, mandrake, savory, skullcap, valerian and vervain.

Fennel Bitters

Prometheus concealed the fire he stole from Olympus in the hollow of a fennel stem (*Foeniculum vulgare*). This plant is a good ally for Virgo to assist in digestion, as its gentle warmth dispels excess gas and fans the flames of the digestive fire. It also alleviates digestive headaches.

The small intestine is ruled by the sign of Virgo, and bitters assist the digestive process by stimulating the liver to produce bile. Digestion is a metabolic process, but also a psycho-spiritual one, signifying how our life experience is assimilated and integrated into our whole.

Energetically, fennel strengthens imaginative and visionary perception, clarifying the mind, and supporting right judgement and discernment in Virgos. It is one of the nine sacred herbs of the Anglo-Saxons thought to ward off demons and protect against enchantment. Pliny the Elder noted that snakes would use fennel juice to shed their skins after hibernation. It is associated with rejuvenation and life-giving powers. As a galactagogue, it increases breast milk, a visceral symbol of life itself.

In the language of flowers, fennel symbolizes reward, power and victory. Champion Olympic athletes and Roman gladiators were often crowned with fennel leaves.

METHOD

1 On Mercury's day (Wednesday), place 2 tablespoons of fennel seeds, 1 tablespoon of dried dandelion root and the dried peel of an orange into a bottle of vodka. To honour Virgo and the goddess of the grain, Demeter, ensure that it is wheat-based. At the bottom, you may also place a crystal of peridot.

2 Put out overnight when the moon is in the sign of Virgo or under the balsamic moon (the dark moon period a few days before a new moon – this is to channel the energies of stillness, reflection and renewal).

3 Leave the bitter remedy for a philosophical month (40 days) and meditate on the process of renewal.

4 Strain and store in a cool, dark place.

APPLICATION

Take as an aperitif or digestif before or after a meal.

Libra

(SEPTEMBER 23–OCTOBER 22)

At the autumn equinox, days and nights once again become equal. We share the harvest, exchanging stories to explore how we relate to each other through the balanced scales of the Libra glyph, the only inanimate symbol in the zodiac. In some versions, Libra was added in to the zodiac to separate Virgo and Scorpio, which were one. The scales represent the Libran quest for balance and harmony. Its esoteric ruler is Uranus, which develops this desire for the progression of humankind. Libra resonates with the alchemical process of sublimation, which is to sublimate and transform lower vibrational and emotional patterns into a higher form through self-awareness and personal evolution. A cardinal sign, it initiates the autumn and a turning inwards, navigating the realism of self and other, and strives to find a balance between them. Libra rules the energetics of the seventh house of love, relationships and romantic partnerships. Just as our souls are weighed against a feather by Anubis after crossing the River Styx into the afterlife, here we must go through a process of refinement and reflection by seeing our truth through the eyes and ears of another. This balance between self and other resides in the air element. Libra is active and primarily hot and moist, although it can also tip the scales and be cold and dry. Its metal is copper and its rulership is exoteric Venus, the goddess of beauty and harmonics. Through its opposite sign, Aries, Libra is given the impetus to move its ideals and ideas towards action.

Libra governs the kidneys, lower (lumbar) back, bladder, ovaries and womb, along with functions of balance, such as the endocrine system and homeostasis of pH in the body (it does this in tandem with Aries, which governs the adrenals).

Libra plants are plants of Venus, with the signatures of fruits, five petals and extravagant beauty. As an air sign, mercurial remedies will balance the nervous system, and Libra's rulership of the kidneys calls for water element remedies, diuretics and alteratives that support the inner waters of the body, urinary and endocrine systems. When the scales tip back and forth, unable to find balance, scleranthus essence is a good aid.

Lemon balm (*Melissa officinalis*) is a plant ally that corresponds to Libra, ruled by Venus and Jupiter. Its name comes from the Greek for 'bee' and 'honey'. Named after the nymph Melissa, this relates to the hive mentality of Librans as social creatures, and the goddess energy of the bee priestesses of Demeter. Considered by Paracelsus to be a cure-all, lemon balm calms the nervous system, heart and digestive tract. In magic, it is used for attraction and love spells. Dandelion (*Taraxacum officinale*) is a key kidney aid for Libra, working as a diuretic and reducing inflammation and restoring balance to the kidneys and urinary tract. The leaves can be cooked, or the flowers made into wine. Crab apple (*Malus sylvestris*) is a tree of Venus and Libra; it tonifies, cleanses and acts as an anti-inflammatory. A flower essence of crab apple is prescribed for low self-image.

Other Libra plants include agrimony, angelica, chamomile, fennel, foxglove, ginkgo, lady's mantle, lavender, linden, meadowsweet, pennyroyal, primrose, rose, sweet violet, tansy, thyme, vervain and yarrow.

Dandelion and Yarrow Wine

Dandelion (*Taraxacum officinale*) is a cleansing bitter plant that stimulates bile production, supporting the liver, gallbladder and digestive system, and cleansing excess earth and water. Its common French name *piss-en-lit* translates as 'wet-the-bed', due to its diuretic properties, which increase urine flow and flush through waste in the kidneys, making it an ideal ally for Libra.

Energetically, it is a seeker and a visionary herb, offering guidance through times of transition and psychic expansion. The seed heads are an emblem of wishes and magic called 'dandelion clocks', as they have long been used tell the time, depending on how many blows it would take for the seeds to disperse, to tell how many lovers one might have, or how many years you will be together. Also called the 'lover's oracle', desires were whispered into it and sent off into the wind to be filtered into their ears and hearts. In the language of flowers, it symbolizes desire and devotion.

Yarrow is a plant of Venus and Libra. It supports this sign as a diuretic, maintaining a healthy urinary tract and homeostasis in reducing inflammation in the kidneys. Energetically, yarrow offers spiritual protection and enhances divinatory potential and psychic awareness. Placed under the pillow while you sleep, it is thought to bring you a vision of your beloved when you wake. It is a strong plant for positive boundaries, both physical and emotional, and promotes courage, dissolving fear and disillusionment.

METHOD

1 Late in the morning on a new moon, before the centre of the flower has woken up, harvest, wash and finely chop the leaves, flowers and roots of young dandelions. Cut one or two handfuls of yarrow leaves.

2 Place the chopped dandelions and yarrow in a jar with a handful of dried apricots or figs, the peel of 1 lemon and 1 orange, ½ cup of brandy and 1 tablespoon of raw honey.

3 Cover with a bottle of red wine and leave to sit until the full moon.

4 Strain into a pan and place an upside-down lid on top. Place some ice on top of the lid, and gently warm to begin circulation distillation. Do this for 8 minutes to honour the orbit of Venus.

5 Bottle and refrigerate.

APPLICATION

Take a small glass of the wine as an aperitif before meals.

Scorpio

(OCTOBER 23–NOVEMBER 21)

As the nights get longer and we move towards Samhain (when the veils between worlds are thinned), Scorpio absorbs the experience of relating to others through Libra and dives deeper into what lies beneath the surface. The eighth house energies of sex, death and the occult are expressed in Scorpio as it purges the shadow, shedding a light on the hidden qualities and conditions within. Ruled by Mars in traditional astrology, Pluto in modern astrology, and again by Mars in esoteric, Scorpio's metal is iron (and, to a lesser degree, plutonium), and it is related to themes of power, will, the element of fire and hidden, underworld forces. It is a fixed sign, and it is the water element in its most dense state as ice: water fixing into the earth. Its energetics are receptive, cold and moist. Scorpio's glyph is similar to that of Virgo, but with the tail turned outward with its sting, where energy is expressed and released in comparison to the internalization of Virgo. Just as Leo's journey is of the self, Scorpio's is of the soul.

Scorpio is associated with alchemical putrefaction and separation, which is the process of descending into the unconscious depths in order to realize what aspects of the shadow need separating from, and how to let go of that which no longer serves. Scorpio governs the eliminatory channels through the colon, bladder, rectum, anus and genitalia. In terms of zodiac polarities, Taurus governs the intake of food through the mouth, and its opposite, Scorpio, governs its excretion through the anus. Imbalances of Scorpio can cause a build-up of toxicity or poisons; digestive stagnation, such as constipation, parasites and infection; and loss or excess of libido and sexually-transmitted diseases. Chicory essence assists Scorpios that may need to lighten up, and vine assists when power becomes an unhealthy drive.

Scorpio plants are Mars and Pluto plants, with thorns or stings that are invasive, growing underground and pungent to taste or smell. They will also have a stimulating and eliminatory effect on the body, warming and quickening elimination, while antipathetic remedies of Venus and the Moon, diuretics and lymphatics purify the inner waters.

Supportive plants like blessed thistle (*Cnicus benedictus*) are an ally of Scorpio. A bitter herb that aids digestion, clearing excess mucus and stagnation, it is used as a remedy to aid drug and alcohol detoxification and rehabilitation. The essence and essential oil are used for protection from toxic situations and releasing old trauma patterns. Walnut (*Juglans regia*) has been used extensively as an antiparasitic, and this is reflected in the way that it tends to kill life around it. A tree of Persephone, it is linked to the underworld and themes of rebirth. Pliny the Elder wrote: 'The shadow of the walnut tree is poison to all plants within its compass.' According to Mrs M. Grieve's *A Modern Herbal*, the bark and leaves of the walnut are alterative, laxative and astringent, and it is a good eliminatory and detoxifying plant for Scorpios. A liquor called nocino is made by tincturing unripe green walnuts in vodka. Similarly, burdock (*Arctium lappa*) will support this eliminatory path.

Other Scorpio plants include barberry, basil, blackberry, blackthorn, ground ivy, lady's mantle, nettles, tarragon, valerian, wormwood and yarrow.

Sloe and Blackberry Vinegar

Bramble (*Rubus fruticosus*) is the letter 'Muin' in the Ogham calendar, the time of the festive harvest, when abundant fruits are picked from the hedgerow and grapes fermented into wine. With the autumn equinox, it signifies community and merriment, before a turning inwards.

In folklore, blackberries should not be picked after Old Michaelmas Day in October, as it was thought that after that, the Devil will spit on them. There is some truth in this, as this is the point at which fungus may form. Blackberries are associated with protection, prosperity and healing, and can assist Scorpios in dispelling negative energies and navigating the underworld, as they are sensitive to shadow forces. Bushes were planted to protect homes from enemies and vampires. In folklore, they were used to protect against spells, break curses, and ward off any psychic attack. Fruits are antioxidant, high in vitamin C, fortifying, strengthening and protective. Leaves are astringent and tighten inflamed bowels.

The Blackthorn tree (*Prunus spinosa*) has strong folkloric associations with Scorpio forces, symbolic of death, protection and revenge. It is the Celtic Ogham of Samhain and represents the balance between light and dark. The blackthorn produces blue-purple berries called sloes.

METHOD

1 Harvest blackberries when the Moon is in Scorpio. Wash and mash them using a pestle and mortar, potentially adding Mars-ruled herbs and spices to taste, such as black pepper, ginger and juniper. Place in a bottle and fill with raw apple cider vinegar – the higher the ratio of blackberries to vinegar, the deeper the flavour. Leave for a week, then strain and bottle.
2 Harvest sloes as late in the season as possible, from when the Sun is 15 degrees Scorpio at astrological Samhain, and preferably after the first frost, when their cell walls become more permeable, their starch converts to sugar, and their tannin content decreases. Prick the flesh a few times and repeat the process above, leaving to steep for two weeks before straining.
3 Combine the two vinegars in a non-reactive pan. Add sugar and the liquid at a ratio of 1:2 sugar to liquid. Bring to the boil and then simmer gently for 10 minutes.
4 Bottle in sterile glass bottles.

APPLICATION

Take a few drops on the tongue, or add 1 teaspoon to hot water as a tonic for the bowels and for protection.

Sagittarius

(NOVEMBER 22–DECEMBER 21)

The nights of reflection and contemplation grow longer as we approach the winter solstice, which celebrates the return of the light, longer days and new possibilities. It is a time to look beyond the horizon, with a fresh perspective gained from the previous months, to sit around the campfire and exchange stories with travellers, and to philosophize and gain new insight. For animals, this is a time for migration. The ninth house is about our spiritual journey, our path to inner truth. Sagittarius is symbolized by a half-human, half-horse centaur and archer, corresponding to higher consciousness, shooting the arrow in search of truth. The glyph for Sagittarius is an arrow pointing skyward. Wild oats essence helps to direct the Sagittarian quest towards its path and channel this into ambition. When this swings the other way and Sagittarius becomes fanatical, vervain essence assists. The last of the fire elements, this is the inner spiritual fire of wisdom. The energetics of Sagittarius are hot and dry and active, and it is a mutable sign. Its metal is tin and its rulership of Jupiter aligns with this sense of expansion and potential. As the philosopher, Sagittarius expresses itself in the outward pursuit of knowledge and truth. Earth is its esoteric ruler, demonstrating the evolution of Sagittarius is to invert this quest, integrating higher wisdom into the material plane by communicating it to the world. Its relationship to its polarity, Gemini, which exists more in the immediate, local world of data, supports this journey of Sagittarius transmuting higher degrees of information back into the now.

Sagittarius energies resonate with the alchemical process of ceration or incineration, a higher octave of the fire forces of Aries' calcination and Leo's digestion. The fire of incineration comes at a later stage of the work, transforming and refining the substance and experience to ashes, with the wisdom of the whole contained in each speck. Sagittarius corresponds to the thighs and hips, upper legs, sciatic nerve, peripheral arteries and autonomic nervous system. Imbalances can cause blood stagnation, inflammation of the nerves,

sciatica, rheumatism and gout. Sagittarius plants are those of Jupiter, and remedial plants are anti-inflammatories, cold and moist herbs, liver tonics and topical herbs for skin and joint complaints. Detoxifying plants like burdock (*Arctium lappa*), dandelion (*Taraxacum officinale*) and chicory (*Cichorium intybus*) that assist in elimination and reduce inflammation are strong supports of Sagittarius. Mercurial herbs to calm the nervous system and relieve muscle spasms and nerve tension are equally beneficial.

Sage (*Salvia officinalis*) is Sagittarius's ally plant, sacred to Jupiter and associated with wisdom and higher learning. As an aromatic bitter, it stimulates digestion through increasing bile and moving congestion through the liver; it also eases nervous headaches and aids rheumatic conditions. As an antispasmodic and antiseptic, the essential oil is used externally to support joints, muscles and skin conditions. The dried herb is burnt and the smoke is used to clear energetic stagnation and raise the vibrations of a space before prayer and ceremony. Devil's claw (*Harpagophytum procumbens*) is used in the treatment of sciatica, due to its anti-inflammatory, diuretic, and anti-rheumatic properties.

Sagittarius plants include agrimony, birch, cedar, chervil, dandelion, eucalyptus, hawthorn, lemon balm, oak, pine, poplar, rosebay willowherb, rowan, samphire and sea buckthorn.

Sea Buckthorn Shrub

Sea buckthorn (*Hippophae rhamnoides*) is a plant that resonates with Sagittarian sentiments in its mythology. The name *hippophae* means 'shiny horse', and it was said to be the favourite food of the mythical flying horse Pegasus.

Another legend has it that the Ancient Greeks released war horses into the wild to die, yet they came back restored after a diet of the miracle berry. Mongol conqueror Genghis Khan is also said to credit the stamina of his army to the 'sacred fruit' of sea buckthorn.

It also supports the liver, ruled by Sagittarius. It is a nutrient-dense superfood rich in antioxidants, vitamins and minerals, and is commonly drunk as a tea in Russia. It encourages movement and flow, and is used as a circulatory tonic because it is restorative, energizing and strengthening. The extracted oil of sea buckthorn is rich in omega oils, and can be used to treat skin conditions and to encourage strong, shiny hair. Energetically, it reveals the warrior within and shows us that, like Pegasus, we can take flight.

METHOD

1 Gather fresh sea buckthorn berries in the midday sun on Jupiter's day (Thursday).
2 Place the berries in a blender and add raw honey and apple cider vinegar in equal parts of 1:1 honey to vinegar, so that the ratio of berries to liquid is 3:2. Blend until smooth.
3 Strain through a muslin cloth. You can save the seeds and return them to the land, or dry them and grind into a powder to use as a seasoning.
4 Add sparking water or soda to complete the shrub.

APPLICATION

Take as a restorative circulatory tonic and digestif.

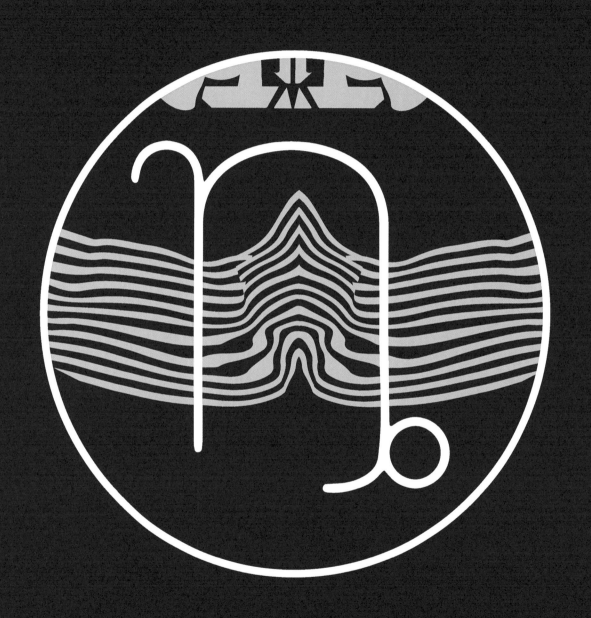

Capricorn

(DECEMBER 22–JANUARY 19)

Capricorn takes the wisdom gained thus far and grounds it into material reality by carving an ambitious and industrious path ahead, conquering the horizons of Sagittarius in the tenth house of career and public status. In Capricorn's glyph, we see its symbol of the sea-goat, a goat with a fish's tail that can move between land and water, and acts as the alchemical mediator, bringing the air and fire elements into the earth through the medium of water. It stands at the top of a cliff, surveying its journey and the wisdom and insight it has gained. The evolution of Capricorn is to transform this wisdom not through ambition for greed or self-interest, but for the greater good of humanity. Capricorn resonates with the alchemical process of fermentation, where the old self decays and the true self emerges, and the spiritualization of matter occurs as we move from Capricorn to Aquarius. As the final earth element in the zodiac, this is the spiritualization of matter. Capricorn's ruler Saturn in both exoteric and esoteric astrology is reflected in the environment with its cooling and contracting nature and its metal being lead, while the cardinal nature of earth initiating the season supports the need for strength of will and perseverance through the winter. Capricorn is cold and dry, receptive and a cardinal sign. With its opposite sign, Cancer, it learns to dance between earth and water, form and feelings. The glyph might also be interpreted as Saturnian forces bending their knees in service of spirit, as this is the transition from the journey of the self to the collective.

Capricorn rules the bones and skeletal system, joints (primarily the knees), skin, hair, nails and structural elements of the body. Imbalances can lead to slow metabolism, stagnation, constriction, weak joints and bones, calcium deficiency and rigidity in mind and body. Hard-working and ambitious, oak and rock water essences support overwork and rigidity of thinking respectively. Remedies include bitters, digestive tonics and plants that are warm and oily to lubricate the system.

Capricorn plants are those of Saturn, and have a tendency to grow out of rocks on cliffs, and in inhospitable places. Mucilaginous mullein (*Verbascum thapsus*) supports Capricorn in remedying cold states, reducing inflammation and strengthening the system as a whole. Topically, it reduces swelling and relieves joint pain. Silica-rich plants such as horsetail (*Equisetum arvense*) and calcium-rich plants such as nettle (*Urtica dioica*) encourage healthy lubrication of the connective tissue, and strong bones and nails. Black mustard (*Brassica nigra*) is an edible plant favoured by goats, and the oil is used for joint and muscle relief, rheumatism and arthritis.

Other Capricorn plants include boneset, comfrey, goatweed, guelder rose, hemlock, horse chestnut, myrrh, plantain, Shepherd's purse, Solomon's seal, sorrel and witch hazel.

Horsetail Spagyric

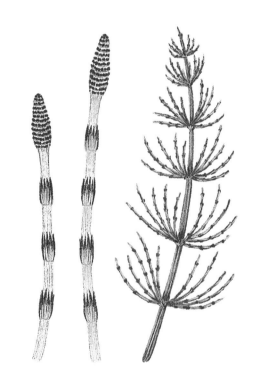

Horsetail (*Equisetum arvense*) is an ancient plant, and is considered a living fossil. It primarily supports connective tissue growth and repair. This is reflected in its structure; it is also called the puzzleplant for the way that it links together.

Silica and calcium are vital for healthy bones, connective tissue, skin, nails and hair, and are found in high quantities in horsetail. Nourishing the structural body, bones and joints, is key for Capricorns. In the doctrine of signatures, rhythmically or symmetrically arranged leaves point towards the musculoskeletal system as it too is arranged rhythmically and symmetrically. As it grows in wet soil near water, horsetail is also used to treat damp conditions in the body. For Capricorns, this may be rheumatoid arthritis. It has a high mineral content helping to fortify the blood, and it works well to tonify places were water lacks a boundary, such as the urinary and genital tracts, where it acts as a diuretic. It expresses a balanced earth element in its support of the earth through water.

In spring, horsetail produces fertile, light brown stems, with a cone-like spore producing structure at the tip. These are traditionally picked and eaten like asparagus. In summer, silica-rich, sterile green shoots develop, which have an appearance like fir trees. As a diuretic, it is the archetype of lubricated earth. Energetically, it helps to connect to the wisdom of the past.

METHOD

1 When the Moon is in an earth sign or Saturn is strong, gather young, fresh horsetail stems in early summer, leaving plenty above the ground for regrowth in sunlight and free of brown fungal spotting. Ensure that you choose a plant that is displaying its full vital force.
2 Place in a jar with brandy or vodka, or ideally a homemade spirit, and hermetically seal.
3 Leave until the full moon in a warm, dark place. Strain the liquid, which now contains the mercurial and sulphuric qualities of the plant, and set aside. Squeeze excess liquid from the plant and place into a pan that can withstand a naked flame at high heat.
4 Set the pan over an open flame, such as a fire pit (oak wood is preferred) or gas camping stove. Do this outside to allow the fumes to disperse and calcify the material into ashes.
5 Place the ashes in a glass with distilled water and filter through a coffee paper.
6 Heat the filtered liquid to evaporate until the ashes appear pure white.
7 Powder the ash using a pestle and mortar and then repeat steps 5 and 6 again, until crystallization occurs and it becomes salt.
8 Combine the salt (while still hot) with the original liquid. Seal in a jar and place outside to deliquesce (to draw the vital force and philosophical fire from the air).
9 Collect just before dawn.

APPLICATION

Take up to 3 drops a day as a restorative tonic, or add a few drops to your bath to support connective tissue and strengthen muscles and joints.

Caution: Not recommended for prolonged use.

Aquarius

The role of Aquarius as the water-bearer is to take the accumulated wisdom acquired on the journey of the zodiac and pour back these inner waters into the earth. This is the middle of winter, a time when we cross the threshold at the midpoint and shift our attention towards spring and the year ahead. The eleventh house is about our role within the collective and wider community, and Aquarius asks us to think differently and to come up with new ideas and inventions so that together, we evolve. In traditional astrology, it is ruled by Saturn, and Uranus in modern, which are reflective of the rebellious, liberated and changeable air element of Aquarius, while also recognizing that in order for change to be enacted, it must be integrated into reality through discipline and the implementation of structures and systems. In esoteric astrology, the ruler of Aquarius is Jupiter, which bestows a desire for the progress, evolution and expansion of humanity to come from a place of benevolence and compassion. Its metals are lead and, to a lesser extent, tin, aluminium and uranium. An air sign, the energetics of Aquarius are active, hot and moist, and it is a fixed sign. Through its polarity, Leo, Aquarius is reminded to bring the abstract, futuristic, detached nature of its quest for humanitarian progress back in to play for human and for heart. The glyph of Aquarius represents both water and air as frequency and vibration. This is the energy that it pours onto Earth. Aquarius is associated with the alchemical process of multiplication; transformation moves from the individual to the multitude, the masses, society as a whole.

Aquarius rules the ankles and calves, Achilles tendon, electrical impulses, nerves and circulation. Imbalanced Aquarians can be ungrounded, aloof and over-idealistic, struggling to focus and in need of the nervines and relaxants of Venus and the Moon. They can also be in need of blood tonics to assist with blood stagnation or poisoning, along with Mercurial nervines to address rhythmic disorders of nerves, circulation and electrical impulses. Plants of Aquarius are Saturnian and Uranian, often with eccentric growth patterns which support the circulatory and nervous system, and they are high in nutrients.

Clary sage essence supports Aquarius in seeing the way forward, and helps in interpreting spiritual and mental insight into an embodied, felt sense. Water violet essence encourages emotionally detached Aquarius to move towards interconnectedness and a deeper heart connection. Stimulants that awaken the senses and clear the mind, such as ginkgo (*Ginkgo biloba*), pine (*Pinus spp.*), ground ivy (*Glechoma hederacea*) and speedwell (*Veronica persica*), help the fixed-air quality of Aquarius with visioning and moving forward. Nervines, such as lavender (*Lavandula angustifolia*), wood betony (*Betonica officinalis*) and passionflower (*Passiflora incarnata*), support an overstimulated and overwhelmed Aquarius. Saturnian herb skullcap (*Scutellaria lateriflora*) is an ally to Aquarius as a nervine and relaxant, drawing the energy down from the head and nourishing exhausted nervous systems. Sweet violet (*Viola odorata*) assists Aquarius in relieving tension in the body that causes headaches and respiratory conditions. It contains rutin and salicylic acid, so is useful in alleviating inflammation as well as bodily aches and pains. It is traditionally made into a syrup.

Other Aquarius plants include barley, bladderwrack, borage, cleavers, clove, Douglas fir, elderberry, fennel, guelder rose, horsetail, linden, mastic, mullein, nutmeg, poppy, spikenard, St John's wort and willow.

Pine and Mullein Fermented Soda

Despite its name, Douglas fir (*Pseudotsuga menziesii*) is not a true fir but a member of the pine family, and has a traditional use in pine needle tea. It is imbibed as an immune-booster, but also for respiratory conditions, coughs, colds, congestion and to improve cognition.

Harvest tender tips in the spring when their citrus-pine flavour is at its strongest. It is best experienced as a simple tea infusion. High in vitamin C, it supports coughs and colds, clears brain fog, hydrates and revives. Its energetics are awakening, uplifting and charging. Pines are associated with immortality and the afterlife, and were placed on temples to underworld god Osiris. They were also considered sacred to the god of the sea, Poseidon, perhaps in connection to the timber being used for ships, and are also linked to Dionysus due to the use of pine in wine-making.

Avicenna credited pine for supporting neuralgia, sciatica and paralysis. Pine supports Aquarius in moving forward, clarifying visions and activating the mind to be able to see beyond the horizon to invoke new ways of being. As a herb of Saturn, mullein (*Verbascum thapsus*) supports the joints and muscles, and helps arthritis caused by air trapped between the joints. Also known as lungwort, the antimicrobial leaves are primarily used as a respiratory tonic taken as a lung tea or steam inhalation, and the flowers are used for ear and nerve conditions. Ceremonial mullein torches – made by dipping the stems in fat – were lit to protect villages, ward off evil spirits and defend against lightning. This symbol of light overcoming shadow corresponds to the Aquarian nature of envisioning the future. Energetically, mullein asks us to turn inwards, and to listen to our inner voice. In the language of flowers, it corresponds to health, positivity and good nature.

METHOD

1 Gather the spruce tips of Douglas fir or Scots pine on a spring day when they are young, and at the time or on the day of Saturn (Saturday).
2 Fill a large jar with the washed tips, leaving a little space at the top, and cover with filtered, non-chlorinated water.
3 Add 1 cup of raw, organic local honey and a handful each of dried mullein flowers and wild berries, such as mulberries.
4 Activate champagne yeast in a separate vessel according to the packet instructions, then add this to the jar and cover with a muslin cloth or tea towel, fixed in place with a rubber band.
5 Keep at room temperature, stirring a few times a day with a non-metallic spoon, looking for signs of healthy fermentation such as bubbles and heat. Depending on the climate, this can take a few days or a week.
6 Strain and bottle, regularly releasing the pressure for the first 24 hours. Refrigerate and consume within a week.

APPLICATION

Drink a glass first thing in the morning to wake up the mind and recalibrate the nervous system for the day.

Pisces

The final sign of the zodiac is Pisces. Leading up to the spring equinox, the environment is in a state of transformation, transitioning out of winter towards summer through the medium of spring. The culmination of the evolutionary expansion of consciousness through all the seasons and growth cycles now enters into a state of intuition, psychic sensitivity, detachment from the physical and the merging back of consciousness into the universe. The twelfth and final house holds our existential longing and desires, and asks what qualities we will hold on to and carry with us into the next life. It is the beginning and the end, and a time of letting go, reflection, expansion and intuitive and psychic guidance. Its glyph of a pair of fishes represents the ocean of cosmic consciousness, our inner waters and the polarities between our lower persona and higher soul. Its exoteric rulers are Jupiter in traditional astrology, and Neptune in modern, which resonate at a level of compassionate idealism. There is a diffusive quality to Pisces; it is at once of this world and beyond it. We might view it as water in the form of steam – a spiritualized water in ethereal form. The esoteric ruler is Pluto, which encourages this level of intuition and idealism to shine light on the suffering of the world and allows it to be revealed and transformed to evolve humanity to a higher octave of being. Its metal is tin, and to a lesser extent plutonium and platinum. Pisces resonates with the alchemical process of projection and the ability to manifest dreams into reality and to project the Philosopher's stone into future processes. It is receptive, mutable, cold and moist. Pisces is the cosmic expression of the earthly love of its opposite sign Virgo, dreaming in the liminal realms rather than of the Earth. Pisces learns to ground through Virgo.

Pisces rules the fluids of the body, particularly the lymphatic and the immune systems, along with the feet. Pisces imbalances are conditions of cold and moist states, congestion in the lungs, oedema and water retention. With a heightened sensitivity and perception, and often weak boundaries, Pisceans can be ungrounded and subject to depression, as well as drawn to drug and alcohol addiction and neurotic disorders and psychic attacks. Willow essence helps to empower Pisceans when sensitivity turns to victimhood, while yarrow offers psychic protection and helps to dispel fear.

Pisces plants are those of Jupiter and Neptune, with strong affiliations with water and expansion. Remedy plants are those that help to ground and direct the inner waters, as well as immuno-modulating herbs that gently stimulate the system and dry out excess damp.

Linden or limeflower (*Tilia* × *europaea*) is a relaxant and sedative that aids sleep and calms the nerves when Pisceans are feeling sensitive. Bladderwrack (*Fucus vesiculosus*) is a seaweed ally for watery Pisces, pulling toxins from the body, cleaning the blood, regulating the thyroid gland, and supporting immune health. Rosehips (*Rosa canina*) are ruled by Jupiter and are an excellent immune tonic, and were called upon during both World Wars to maintain a healthy population.

Silver birch (*Betula pendula*) is usually the first sap to flow, heralding spring and symbolizing rebirth, nourishment and protection. Its waters are deeply cleansing as a diuretic anti-inflammatory, removing excess earth built up during the winter months. It supports Pisces in cleansing the lymph. Other Pisces plants include bilberries, chickweed, cleavers, geranium, lotus, lungwort, meadowsweet, mugwort, neroli, poppy, red clover, willow, wood betony and yarrow.

Red Clover and Cleavers Lemonade

Red clover (*Trifolium pratense*) is a nutritive herb that supports lymphatic function and the inner waters of the female reproductive system to balance hormones. It is used for menopausal hot flushes and hormone-related skin conditions.

It is also used as a blood cleanser and calming nervine. Energetically, it symbolizes love, fidelity and abundance. It assists with psychic expansion and journeying. It can also be symbolic of farewell and endings, and was planted on graves as a mark of the resurrection. Its leaves are a sign of the power of three. In the language of flowers, the clover symbolizes desire, both carnal and spiritual. The red clover specifically means a hunger for love and fidelity. Clover's introduction into playing cards as the suit of clubs is thought to represent a tryst between the King, Queen and Jack; for this reason, it is also thought to mean promises or revenge.

Cleavers (*Galium aparine*) is a key Pisces ally due to its properties as a lymphatic tonic and as a soothing, anti-inflammatory diuretic that can be used to cleanse the kidneys and urinary tract, and treat skin conditions. *Galium* comes from the Greek for 'milk', as it was used to curdle cheese. Its other common name, bedstraw, is on account of its use to stuff mattresses. It can be used as a blood-cleansing spring tonic to flush out winter debris, and calm swollen glands and the inner waters of the nervous system and emotional body. Energetically, cleavers encourages healthy boundaries, non-attachment and non-clinging in relationships.

METHOD

1 Gather red clover flowers on Jupiter's day (Thursday) or under a Pisces moon.
2 Create an infusion by covering the flower heads with water and gently bringing to the boil. Remove from the heat and allow to cool slightly before adding raw local honey to taste. Let it steep for 10 minutes, then strain and bottle.
3 Gather fresh young cleavers leaves and stems and pack into a jug, filling it with water. If you have tapped and frozen birch sap during Pisces season, its immune and cleansing functions make it an ideal addition here (see page 63). Add fresh mint, basil or other wild aromatic herbs, and place in the fridge overnight.
4 Strain and combine the two mixtures at a ratio of 1:20 syrup to cleavers. Add the juice of a lemon and top up with soda or sparkling water.

APPLICATION

Drink as a lymphatic tonic and to clarify the internal energetic waters.

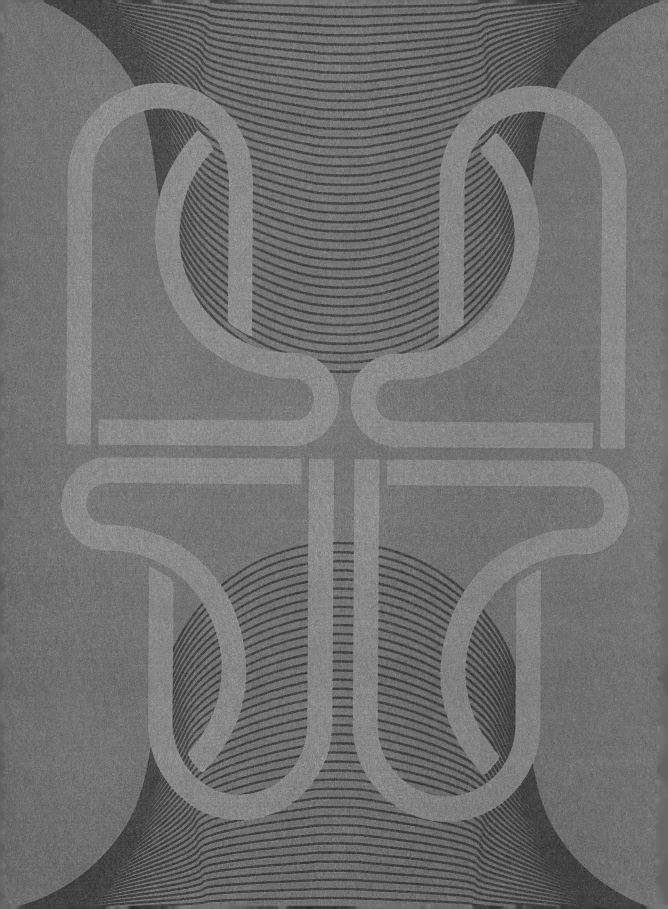

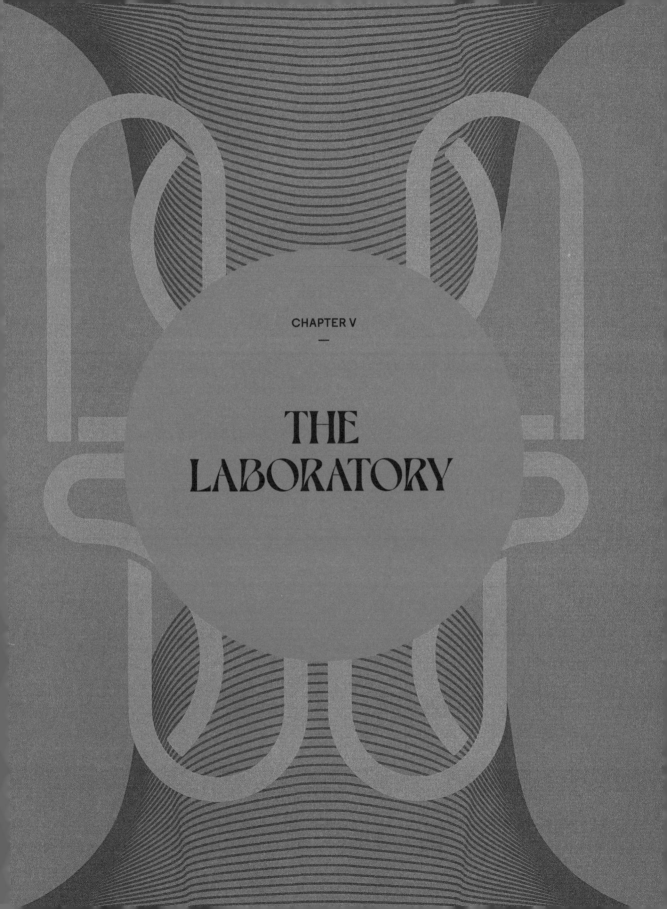

CHAPTER V

—

THE
LABORATORY

Ora et Labora

The experience of the laboratory is an extension of the sacred communion of the wild, and is in alignment with nature and the cosmos. It is where the inner and outer worlds of the alchemist conjoin and create a third dimension, which is the ground for magical transformation. The word laboratory comes from the phrase *ora et labora*, meaning 'to pray and to work'. These two aspects were considered as the intuitive, lunar intelligence of the heart (*ora*) and the thinking, physical masculine (*labora*), representing the right and left hemispheres of the brain. The marriage of the two creates the alchemical child, separating the puffers from the alchemists. In order to apply the alchemical process through labour, it is first required to create a high vibrational and purified state of receptivity and openness where cosmic consciousness can be distilled into physical endeavour. Beyond the beakers and flasks and stills and crucibles, the laboratory of an alchemist contains an altar where sigils, talismans, crystals and sacred herbs are burnt to purify the space to protect from low vibrational fields and external influence, and to maintain sacred connection. The alchemists understood what quantum physics now calls 'the observer effect', and its influence on the result of quantum phenomena. This is the level at which the conscious alchemist is functioning: as a vibrational architect.

MAGIC AND RITUAL

The role of magic (can also be spelled 'magick' to differentiate spiritual or metaphysical magic from stage illusionism) and ritual that developed alongside human evolution and that is present in an alchemical approach incorporates the elemental forces, the language of nature and the energetic matrix of matter. The use of formulae or spells takes the spoken word and the ability for thought forms to shape an energetic or vibrational force capable of informing a state of being. Symbols, sigils, talismans, dream pillows and amulets holding specific energetic charges alter the energetic frequency of a remedy or situation, creating resonance or dissonance. Herbal scrying is the process of pouring out a layer of dried or powdered herbs and, with closed eyes, allowing your hand to draw freely a symbol from your subconscious. The creation of a formula or spell requires first for an intention to be made, then for the caster to calculate the appropriate timing, and gather the energies – inner and outer – along with the plants and any tools required.

Meditate, align your heart with the highest intentions, clear the energies of the laboratory, and make the necessary offerings. Then, through intuition or guidance, find the appropriate words and cast them out into the universe, releasing the energies to their destination. Once complete, there is an exchange and acknowledgment of gratitude, and the ceremonial space is closed.

SETTING UP

Find a place to create an altar with a censer and charcoal where you can burn herbs before you begin your work to purify the space. Make your immediate environment a sacred space. These can be fresh or dried plants, chosen depending on your intention, or sacred tree resins such as frankincense or myrrh. Lay out a space for processing herbs, with access to filtered water, a sink and a naked flame. Create an altar honouring the elements.

CONTAINERS

In alchemy, copper, iron and stainless-steel pots are used, never aluminium. In traditional herbalism and when making spagyrics (see page 178), it is advisable to use glass and ceramics so as not to damage compounds through oxidation, as reactive metals can cause metallic oxides. Avoid non-stick pots due to the chemical coating which, when scratched, can release toxins or aluminium that can leach out and contaminate the remedy. Herbs and remedies can be stored in a range of brown, green or blue glass jars to protect them from degradation by UV light. Jars and vessels should always be sterilized before use.

HERMETIC SEAL

A hermetic seal is an airtight seal that is achieved by sealing a vessel using dough, clay, putty or electrical tape.

'Be quiet in your mind, quiet in your senses, and also quiet in your body. Then, when all these are quiet, don't do anything. In that state truth will reveal itself to you.'

KABIR

LAB EQUIPMENT

Alembic still
Aquatic water pump
Basket
Beakers
Bung and airlock
Capsule machine
Censer
Charcoal discs
Coffee grinder
Crucible
Dehydrator or mesh dryer
Demijohn
Double boiler
Droppers and pipettes
Elastic bands
Enamel and glass bowls
Enamel and metal pots
Fermentation bucket
Glass cucurbit
Grater
Japanese tea infuser
Jars and containers
Knife (for cutting and ceremonial uses)
Labels
Measuring cups, teaspoons and jars
Muslin cloths
Pans
Percolator
Pestle and mortar
Scales
Scissors
Siphon tubing
Slow cooker
Thermometer
Tongs
Trowel

APOTHECARY ESSENTIALS

Alcohol
Brewer's yeast or champagne yeast
Butters, such as shea, cocoa and soy
Carrier oils
Dried herbs
Essential oils
Flower and crystal essences
Hydrosols
Oil infusions
Raw apple cider vinegar
Raw honey
Salts
Sterilization tablets
Sugars
Tinctures
Vegetable glycerin and capsules
Waxes, such as bee, soy and candelilla

Great mullein (*Verbascum thapsus*).

PROCESSING

When returning from foraging, separate, clean and dry your plants, taking care not to bruise the material by using a sharp knife or scissors. Depending on their properties, they may need specific processes; for example, acorns need rinsing repeatedly to release the highly concentrated tannins.

Plants should be processed as soon as possible after picking, while their vital force is pure and potent, particularly if using fresh botanicals for a remedy. The potency of some herbs becomes concentrated and intensified though drying, and these are used as tea infusions, tinctures or powders. Herbs should be dried in dark, dry and well-ventilated environments with good air circulation. Traditionally, small posies are tied together tightly by the stem and hung upside down in brown paper or thin cloth bags to catch debris and seeds. It is also possible to use mesh screens in dry environments, a dehydrator or an oven on the lowest setting with the door open. Herbs are only ever dried in direct sunlight for alchemical and magical purposes when the energetics of the Sun are required, as sunlight breaks down many chemical constituents. Drying times will depend on the humidity of the environment and the water content of the plant itself, which will be influenced by its botanical structure, lunar phase and also the recent weather conditions. The water content will differ amongst parts of the plant itself, so these will have different drying times, and it may make sense to separate the parts for consistent drying so as not to over-dry some parts while under-drying others. Consider retaining some seeds for seed banking or returning them to the land.

WATER

Filtered spring water should be used, as tap water may contain contaminants such as heavy metals and pharmaceutical drugs, only a fraction of which are removed by standard filtration such as charcoal. In alchemy, water collected during a lightning storm is prized as the *prima materia* of water, thought to be condensed starlight, channelled through the magnetism of intention and charged with the forces of nature and the cosmos. Alchemical and vibrational remedies rely on the quantum structure of water to retain the vibrational essence of its surroundings and all that it comes into contact with. Distillation of water is thought to reset this, making distilled water a blank canvas for remedies. Water can be restructured through the application of flower or crystal essences, meditation, sound (by placing it on a sigil or symbol), or by placing it out in the moonlight, depending on the intention for the remedy.

LIQUIDS

Use high-grade oils that are organic and free of chemicals and pesticides, cold–pressed if possible. In modern herbalism, medical-grade ethanol – 96% or 100% proof – is used and diluted with water to around 35%, but this requires a license in most countries, so instead a minimum 40% volume vodka or brandy is traditionally used (40% volume = 40% alcohol and 60% water).

RATIO

Ratios provide a basic formula and represent the relationship between ingredients. Understanding this dance and some of the chemistry and culinary reactions involved provides a true understanding of the nature of a formula and liberates the alchemist from rigid thinking. It allows nature to take the lead, avoiding over-harvesting and creating a visual and intuitive space that allows for recipes and remedies to be easily scaled up or down. Ratios may be worked out by individual quantity, weight, volume or eye. If you require scales to measure small amounts – such as 5g of beeswax, jeweller's scales are most appropriate.

LONGEVITY

Over time, dried herbs and powders will visibly lose their vital force through discoloration and loss of odour. Liquids will gain foam or mould, and oils will go rancid and have a musty odour. However, not all contaminants are visible, so use appropriate care in processing and storage. In general, infusions, decoctions and water-based remedies can be kept for up to 3 days. Alcoholic tinctures and vinegars will last up to 2 years. Syrups can be kept for 2 weeks to 2 months, depending on their sugar content. Honey with fresh plants can be kept for 6 months, or with dried plants for up to a year, and, fermentations and brews for up to 2 weeks. Oils, creams and balms can be kept for 6 months to a year. Refrigerate liquid remedies, with the exception of alcoholic tinctures, vinegars, oils and balms. Store all botanicals in airtight jars.

TIMING

Unless making a special remedy, avoid eclipses for 48 hours on either side. Give drying and warming remedies ideally when the Moon is passing through fire signs, and cooling and moistening ones when the Moon is passing through the water signs. In general, avoid the late balsamic or dark moon, which has a depleting energy. Purgative remedies are best given when the Moon is transiting a water sign, as this encourages flow. There may be more sensitivity or reaction to remedies when the Moon is transiting a fire sign. Nourishing, building and tonifying remedies are best used during the waxing moon, and purgative, eliminative remedies during the waning moon. Food preservation should be avoided in the signs of the bowels, heart and head, except drying, when the fire signs are supportive. Pickling and fermenting is done on flower (air) and fruit (fire) days, and canning in water signs. Tinctures are often made on the new moon and strained on the full moon. As the Moon waxes, it draws out the medicinal properties into the alcohol, but once it starts to wane, the properties will begin to return to the plant material.

LABELLING

Processed plants can be tricky to identify, as they lose their colour, smell and physical appearance, particularly when dried, so label them as soon as possible. It is good practice to list the common and botanical names, the part used, the date gathered and the planetary ruler or primary elemental correspondence. For tinctures, you should also add the ratio.

PARTS USED KEY:

Cort. (*cortex* = bark)
Fruct. (*fructus* = fruit)
Flos (*flos* = flower)
Rad. (*radix* = root)
Sem. (*semen* = seed)
Fol. (*folium* = leaf)
Herba (*herba* = aerial parts/leaves)

Example: *Sambucus nigra* (fruct.) 1:4 25%, denotes a tincture of elder (fruit), 1 part by weight to 4 parts by volume of water/ethanol, 25% ethanol strength. Venus, Water, Air.

'Use no strong medicines, if weak will serve the turn, you had better take one too weak by half, than too strong in the least.'

CULPEPER

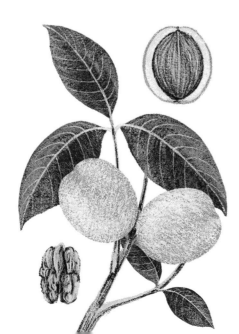

Walnut (*Juglans regia*).

Formula Creation

Primary factors to consider when making a formula are strength and location of symptoms, individual constitution, quality of the condition according to the elements and whether it is chronic or acute, the psycho-spiritual and its planetary influences, and root systems of elimination and rejuvenation. The treatment approach may be sympathetic or antipathetic, or a combination of herbal influences that reflect the complexities of the energetic constitution.

Chemical reactions in living systems are controlled by complex protein enzymes like pepsin and pancreatin, which act as organic catalysts and ensure that reactions are energy efficient. From a phytochemistry perspective, we can categorize herbal actions as either catalysts that accelerate enzyme function, or synergistic, working in harmony with other components to enhance overall effect, such as piperine in black pepper, which improves the bioavailability of certain plants like turmeric. Inhibitors stop an action or reaction, and activators more generally support or protect enzyme activity. For example, magnesium is required for phosphate transfer, and zinc is necessary for vitamin C absorption.

The dominant herb(s) are those that directly address the purpose of the formula. Supporting herbs are those that support the action of the main herb. An assisting herb is one that treats associated symptoms and enhances the effects of the main herbs and the supporting herbs. Carrier herbs are used to carry the other herbs throughout the body to the required location and to improve the flavour of the herbs or aid their digestion and assimilation. A balancing herb is used to balance, soften or ease the action of the dominant herb and mitigate any side effects or extreme states.

ELEMENTAL BALANCE

An elemental formula will take into account the balance of the elements within a person. A remedy might be approached in the balance of constituents. For example, more tannins, sugars, fixed oils, proteins, amino acids, minerals and bitter compounds may be used for earth; more volatile oils and astringents for air; acids and flavonoids for fire; and mucilaginous polysaccharides for water. A remedy might be made of specific parts of the plant – the leaves for water, the flowers for fire. A full-spectrum earth remedy might look at each of the elements within the earth – the physical earth of earth, but also the emotional water of earth, and the thinking air of earth. The individual preparations may also correspond to the timing of the elements – air as dawn, fire as noon, water as dusk and earth as night. The entire life cycle of a plant may be captured over the course of a year as it develops with each season.

For example, the leaves, blossom then berries and bark of hawthorn are picked in the spring, summer and autumn to be made into an elixir.

ASTROLOGICAL BALANCE

An astrological formula builds on the foundation of the elements and looks to the planetary rulerships of each of the *tria prima* levels of an issue or person – the body, spirit and soul – and addresses all three to varying degrees. Then we consider the astrological matrix of a person based on their natal chart, and the rulership of a plant, which will inform the timing of cultivation, remedy-making and taking of the treatment.

DOSAGE

The higher the percentage of plant material in a remedy, the more potent it will be. Dry herbs are more concentrated than fresh. Dosage varies according to the individual and the plant, but unless in the acute, it is wise to start gently and build up as required. Things take time to evolve, and it is only through listening to our bodies and truly knowing ourselves that we are able to measure and adjust dosage and to effectively witness the healing process as a gradual, evolutionary change on all levels. It is particularly the most profound subtle level that requires discernment. It is also part of knowing when to take time to integrate and to allow the body to rest and digest its experience. Remedies should not be taken for prolonged periods of time unless specified. As a general rule, infusions using 1–2 teaspoons of fresh or dried herbs per cup of water can be taken up to 3 times a day. For tinctures, ½–1 teaspoon diluted in water can be taken up to 3 times a day. Syrups are taken in doses of 2 teaspoons per day up to three times a day.

Preparations

Powdered herbs provide increased bioavailability while retaining the full spectrum of nutrition in the whole plant. They can be put into vegetable capsules or rolled into pills or electuaries with honey or similar fatty binding agents such as coconut oil, that will also assist in absorption in the digestive tract. Pastilles or lozenges act like time capsules, allowing for the active properties of plants to coat the mucous surfaces of the mouth, throat and upper respiratory tract. Demulcent mucilaginous herbs like marshmallow root are naturally binding, so ideal for this purpose, along with herbs for calming and soothing; they are prepared by blending with honey into balls or discs and then air-dried. To prevent sticking and add flavour, dust with a powder like rosehip. A poultice is used externally for topical applications of herbs and made by moistening herbs with water or oil so that they come together; the constituents are activated and readily transferred, then strained and bundled into a carrier. This can be a thin muslin cloth, or the herbs can be made into a paste using flour or honey. A simple example of the poultice principle is an insect bite or rash when you are in nature. Pick a few plantain leaves and chew them in your mouth, then spit out and apply directly to the skin. Birch polypore is an excellent field plaster. A fomentation or compress is a hot or cold infusion or decoction applied to the skin via a cloth.

SIMPLE EXTRACTIONS

Benefits of whole herb preparations are that the full spectrum of the plant and its energetics are maintained, as well as the medical qualities of its unadulterated taste. However, it may not be assimilated in the body this way, and some properties require extraction. For example, a tincture will enter the bloodstream quicker, and some whole herbs are hard for the body to process, particularly if one is convalescing or not accustomed to botanical medicine.

Breaking down a plant increases its surface area so that it can be better absorbed. With extractions, the liquid used to draw out active principles can better penetrate the plant material. The methods used will be guided by the nature of a plant and the water solubility of its constituents. The primary crude methods are infusions and decoctions. Some plants will dissolve in water (infusions or percolations), others will require alcohol (tincture), some require a dilution of water and alcohol (fluid extract), some benefit from oil (macerate) and others that are high in volatile oils require distillation (steam condensation). Gemmotherapy extracts use the seeds, young buds, shoots or root tips to capture the full potential of the part contained in these initial stages.

DISTILLATIONS

Distillation replicates the alchemical and elemental process within nature and our weather. Fire heats the earth, releasing water into the air as steam and carrying with it the volatile oils held within the plant. These are then cooled and condensed. The volatile oils are the essential oils, and the fragrant flower water is the hydrosol, which is often used as a spray or added to bath water, and is subtle but uplifting. Essential oils are transcellular, so can travel through the cell membrane and penetrate the body within 20 minutes of application.

DECOCTIONS

Decoctions are used for hard, dense plant material, such as roots and barks, by bringing the herb to the boil in water before simmering gently for around 30 minutes, then standing for another hour or overnight, depending on the herb. A slow cooker also works well for this. If creating a blend, add the hardest parts first and the delicate parts later. Keep the lid on to prevent the essential oils from escaping. Soak tough roots in cold water overnight first.

DIGESTION

A hot infusion, tea or tisane is made by steeping delicate plant material such as leaves and flowers in boiling water for 10–20 minutes, although this can sometimes be longer or shorter as some herbs become very bitter quickly. The plants should never boil as this degrades the vitamins and minerals. Instead, pour the boiling water over the herbs and allow them to stand. Hot infusions draw out vitamins, enzymes and aromatic volatile oils. For a hot infusion, the standard proportions are 1 part ground dried herbs (twice that for fresh herbs) to 20 parts boiling water – the equivalent of 1 teaspoon to a cup. Using a teapot or a pot with a lid keeps the volatile oils contained. A French press can also be used. Herbs are generally taken this way up to three times a day.

MACERATIONS

A cold infusion is when herbs are steeped in cold water. These are usually delicate, such as cleavers, or mucilaginous, such as mallow, as mucilage is damaged by heating. Cold infusions also retain considerably more of the properties of volatile oils, whereas these properties are soon airborne, and thus lost, in hot infusions. Steep overnight. As many herbs appropriate for cold infusions have a relationship to the Moon, leaving them to infuse in the moonlight activates and potentizes these lunar forces.

PERCOLATION

Herbs are dried and powdered, increasing their surface area and allowing for soluble constituents to be rapidly extracted in a 24-hour period. Rinse the powder in liquid (either water or alcohol, depending on the plant constituents and desired outcome), then place and pack down in the percolator cone with a filter. Pour liquid gently over the powder, working in stages, until it is saturated and it begins to drip into the container vessel.

INFUSIONS

Herbs can be infused into the skin with a herbal bath. Add 1 litre of herbal decoction into the bath along with a handful of salts for assimilation. Alternatively, fresh herbs can be placed in a small cloth bag to act as a tea bag. Fresh seaweed placed directly in the bath nourishes and tonifies. Add flower and crystal essences or hydrosols for a full-spectrum remedy.

CONCENTRATES

A concentrate is either an infusion or a decoction that is brought close to a boil, and then gently simmered until it is one-half of its original volume.

SYRUPS

A syrup can be made by adding herbs to raw honey, which is antibacterial and acts as a preservative. Honey's antiseptic properties and consistency coats mucous membranes and allows herbs to effectively be absorbed, making it an ideal remedy for coughs and sore throats. Syrups are essentially cordials, although traditionally these were heart tonics and were intended to strengthen and increase the vital force within. Local and small-batch beekeepers that ensure the vitality of their bees will elicit a higher quality syrup. Honey should remain below body temperature when it is added to either a warm decoction or concentrate. The amount can be gauged by consistency and taste. It is also possible to create a syrup using a 2:1 ratio of raw granulated sugar to water, and heating on the stove until

dissolved. This, with the addition of the liquid extract, can be taken alone or added to other drinks or infusions.

VIBRATIONAL REMEDIES

Vibrational remedies rely on the energetic signature of a plant – its essence – rather than the material content of the plant. Remedies are 'charged' with the frequency of the plant and, when ingested, the body receives this information on a subtle level. These can be essences made of flower, mushrooms and crystals or homeopathic remedies. Homeopathic remedies are made by taking the mother tincture (liquid extraction) and diluting it 1 part to 99 parts alcohol, then shaking. This yields a 1C potency (one part per hundred). This process is repeated to remove the gross material substance until only the subtle vibrational signature is left. Each time this practice of dilution and succussion occurs (trituration), the signature becomes intensified and more potent, with each step yielding a more dilute (gross) but more potent (subtle) remedy.

LUMINARY WATERS

Moon water is water charged under the light of a full moon. Made using rain collected during a full moon in a silver or glass bowl, it is made for use on the body part that is ruled by the zodiac sign the Moon is in. This can be used alone, or as the basis for more complex remedies. Similarly, Sun water can be made in a glass or gold vessel, either as a generic zodiac sign when the Sun is at 15 degrees or as a specific remedy made when the Sun is at the same degree as it was at your birth.

ESSENCES

Flower essences are vibrational liquid extracts. They help us to reframe our mental processes so that we can transcend our emotional responses and conditioning and see things from a fresh perspective.

Essence-making begins with a meditation with the chosen plant, offering gratitude and establishing an exchange. Two methods are traditionally used to prepare flower essences: the sun method and the boiling method.

THE SUN METHOD

This is the most common method. It must be performed on a clear, sunny day, with flowers in their prime.

- Fill a glass bowl with purified spring water and nestle it as close to the plant as possible.
- Cut flowers close to the base and collect them in a basket, or let them fall straight into the bowl from the plant. (Where it is possible to do so, the flowers can be bent into the bowl, rather than cut.)
- Use tweezers or tongs to arrange the flowers face up, covering the surface of the water, and leave to sit in direct sunlight for 3–4 hours. No shadow should fall onto the bowl, including that of the creator. (The creator's role is to facilitate and to hold space for the energetic transfer of the essence of the plant into the structure of the water, not to influence it.)
- Carefully remove the flowers with tongs or tweezers and strain the liquid through a fine mesh. Return the flowers to the plant as an offering.
- Follow the mother essence steps (right).

THE BOILING METHOD

Woodier plants, and those that bloom when the sun is weak, are generally prepared using the boiling method.

- Harvest the flowers and twigs. Place them in a pot of purified spring water and boil for up to 30 minutes. Leave to cool.
- Carefully remove the plant material with tongs or tweezers. Strain the liquid through a fine mesh. Return the flowers to the plant as an offering.
- Follow the mother essence steps (right).

As you deepen your practice, and your sensitivity to energy fields increases, you will get a feel for the subtle energetics of plants and realize that they do not conform to rigid structures. You can then try making essences using the energetics method.

THE ENERGETIC METHOD

- Place a bowl or bottle of purified spring water next to a plant and invite it to share its energy with the water.
- You will get a sense of when the exchange happens between a plant and the water as you feel the transformative shift. It is an 'aliveness' that can even be witnessed in the visual clarity and refraction of light through the water. There is also merit to making essences under the moonlight, at dawn or dusk, or during a storm, depending on the desired outcome.
- Follow the mother essence steps (top right).

MOTHER ESSENCES AND DILUTION

Once you have your essence, you need to mix the energized water with alcohol. This will act as a preservative and lock in the vibrational blueprint of the plant. Brandy or vodka are traditionally used, at a 1:1 ratio with the essence. This creates the mother essence.

The mother essence can be used to 'prove' the remedy, to experience its effects and potency. It is then further diluted by adding 2–10 drops (use your intuition; there is no right or wrong) to a 60ml (¼ cup) stock bottle filled with purified spring water and alcohol at a ratio of 1:1. The dilution of the essence depends on the sensitivity of the individual: most people benefit from a regular application of a diluted essence over an extended period of time, although a single dose may be enough for some. Repeat the dilution process, adding 2–4 drops of essence if required.

The diluted essences are taken either by placing a few drops under the tongue, or added to water and sipped. This can be done up to 4 times a day. In acute situations, such as shock, essences may be taken hourly.

OIL MACERATIONS

Olive oil and borage oil are anti-inflammatory, sesame oil is warming, rosehip oil is high in antioxidants, sunflower oil is nourishing and almond oil supports immune function. For an oil maceration, plant material (partially or fully dried) is steeped in warm or room-temperature oil, such as olive, sunflower, almond or sesame oil, to transfer the volatile oils and active constituents from the plant into the oil. If the herb is delicate, room-temperature oil should suffice. Hardier plant parts may require warm oil. Add the herb and oil to a jar at a ratio of 1:5 herb to oil. It may be necessary to add more oil after the first day, once the initial amount has been absorbed, to create full saturation, as plant matter must be submerged with a good inch of oil on top. Fresh herbs should be wilted for a day or so before being added to the oil, and it is important that there is no water left in the oil at the end or it will go rancid.

Leave the jar sealed in a container that protects the contents from UV rays but is exposed to the heat of the Sun. The timing for this is around 7–10 days. Some plants with strong solar rulership can be exposed to sunlight, such as St John's wort oil.

A salve or balm can be made by mixing herbal oil with melted wax (traditionally beeswax, though there are other plant-based wax alternatives) with a ratio of 4:1, oil to wax. Herbal oils made with fresh herbs are for external use only, due to the risk of botulism.

TINCTURES

A tincture uses alcohol to break down the cellular structure and pulls out the active ingredients of plant matter. It also dissolves non-aqueous solvents and acts as a preservative. The liquid or solvent part of the macerating tincture is called the menstruum, and the solid plant material is called the marc. Brandy was traditionally used in many remedies, although modern brandy is often quite adulterated with preservatives and additives, so ensure it is of high quality from a small distillery. Gin is made up of grain alcohol flavoured with juniper and other botanicals that will influence the remedy. Vodka tends to be purer, but brandy does have a more grounding energy than vodka.

Some very delicate plants, like rose and lemon balm, only need around 12 hours, particularly with rose as the tannins become strong.

To make a tincture, break up the fresh plant material and place into a bottle, then cover with alcohol. Ensure that the liquid covers the plant material, allowing at least an inch above the top. Using dried herbs instead of fresh will create a stronger tincture, as there will be greater ratio of material to liquid. The standard definition of a tincture is a 1:4 ratio of herb to menstruum. In practice, a range of ratios are used, with 1:5 or 1:10 ratios being most common.

Leave the sealed bottle in a warm dark space, unless working with solar forces, in which case a windowsill might be appropriate. It is also possible to take it out each night to bath in the moonlight or to bury it in the earth, perhaps close to the plant or tree of its origin to enhance energetics. Shake the bottle every few days and ensure that the plant material is always submerged beneath the liquid, as the plant material can expand initially, and when it comes into contact with the air it, can decompose and go mouldy.

Tinctures are taken in doses of 1 teaspoon, up to three times a day. Even just a few drops of tincture can have a profound impact on our physical and emotional wellbeing. For children or those sensitive to alcohol, tinctures can be dropped into hot water and the alcohol allowed to evaporate first. Alternatively, they can be made with vegetable glycerin, oil or vinegar.

HERBAL BITTERS

Herbal bitters encourage appetite and aid digestion by stimulating the pancreas to secrete digestive enzymes and the liver to increase flow of bile. Traditional digestive bitters are made of 1 part dried botanicals to 5 parts alcohol (minimum 40%), or 1 part fresh botanicals to 2 parts alcohol.

GLYCERITES

Vegetable glycerin is excellent for use with herbs that are high in tannins, but will not work for extracting fixed oils (fatty oils that are not volatile) or resins. These are made according to the tincture method. 60% glycerin is often added to other tinctures as a preservative. Glycerin is very sweet, so it can destroy the bitter taste principle. Raw apple cider vinegar may be used instead of alcohol or glycerin, although this is a less potent method with less longevity. Adding a little glycerin to the apple cider vinegar will help to extend shelf life.

HERBAL VINEGARS

Herbal vinegars are made by combining herbs with the medicinal properties of raw vinegar, and are made using the tincturing process. Cover the plant material completely with vinegar, shake every few days and strain after a fortnight.

OXYMELS

An oxymel is made by mixing the herbal vinegar with raw honey at 1:4 ratio of vinegar to honey.

HERBAL WINES

A herbal wine infusion is traditionally made using sherry or port due to their high alcohol content, although a biodynamic or organic wine from a small vineyard is a good alternative. A remedy used by the ancient Egyptians was blue lotus (*Nymphaea caerulea*) wine, which has psychoactive properties and was used for meditation and rituals. Wines and beers can also be made directly from plants including gorse, dandelion and elderflower. Mead made from honey adds another dimension with its healing properties and the sacred energetics of bees.

ELIXIRS

Elixirs are alchemical preparations that are aligned with the cosmos, and formulated to integrate the movements of the luminaries, stars and planets. Herbal tonics are remedies of a combination of plants balanced to help restore, tone and invigorate systems in the body and strengthen overall. An elixir targets a specific organ, body system or area that is unbalanced. These remedies have a physical, mental, emotional and spiritual aspect to them, and so can penetrate deeper into the healing nature of the subject, offering the potential for transformative states.

FLUID CONDENSERS

To make a fluid condenser, simmer herbs in water with the lid on for 20 minutes. Cool then strain, and repeat the process once more before leaving to cool. Then add equal parts alcohol to the liquid, along with a pinch of 24-carat gold flakes. Take a drop as required. Its purpose is dependent on the herb, but will always channel the qualities of the Sun.

EXTRACTING THE QUINTESSENCE AND MAKING A SPAGYRIC

The goal of advanced alchemical practice is to release the quintessence of a plant and integrate it into a remedy. When this is done at its highest virtue, it is known as the *primum ens*. The primary methods applied in alchemical practice are digestion, either through the breakdown and extraction of matter through putrefaction (fermentation) or maceration (dissolving in liquid), and circulation – involving two joined cucurbits that allow for the circulation of plant vapour and liquids up and out and then back into the plant matter. All of this is in preparation for distillation (separating volatile oils from plant waters) and sublimation (changing a substance from solid into gas). Once the gas, oils and liquids (mercury and sulphur) have been separated from the plant matter (salt), the latter is calcified to ashes and then all components are recombined into a superior liquid of the plant quintessence, known as a spagyric. A spagyric acts on all three levels of the *tria prima*. Tinctures are considered the short path, while spagyrics are the long path. Whereas it is normal practice to discard the plant matter after making and filtering a tincture, a spagyric recognizes this as the salt element and seeks to recombine it with the sulphur and mercury forces (the essential oils and ethanol-alcohol, respectively). Once all three elements are recombined, you have the highest expression of the plant manifested into physical form.

Vervain (*Verbena officinalis*).

'The flower is a cosmic attractor. An ephemeral unstable body that allows one to perceive – that is, to absorb, the world.'

EMANUELE COCCIA

Glossary

ALCHEMICAL TERMS

· Albedo – the whitening stage of separation and conjunction.
· Alembic still – apparatus for the distillation of liquids, traditionally made of copper, comprising of a pot containing the substance to be distilled, heated underneath, and a domed cap to collect the rising vapours, which are then cooled via a condenser and collected as liquid in a receiver.
· Bain-marie – double-boiler, hot-water bath.
· Calcination – heating a substance with fire to reduce to ashes.
· Celestial niter – creates fixed elements of earth and water from *prima materia*.
· Celestial salt – creates volatile elements of fire and air from *prima materia*.
· Ceration – softening a hard substance through the addition of heat and liquid.
· Circulation distillation – the heating of a substance to cause it to evaporate, recondense and re-evaporate continuously.
· Citrinitis – the yellowing stage of putrefaction and fermentation.
· Coagulation – precipitation of distillation, changing state from gas or liquid into solid or semi-solid state.
· Congelation – process of crystallization.
· Conjunction – reconstitution of elements of separation (*see* separation).
· Cucurbit – vessel or flask containing liquid for distillation, used with or as part of alembic.
· Digestion – gentle heat is applied to a substance over a long period of time.
· Dissolution – dissolving of ashes in water.
· Distillation – boiling and condensing of a solution.
· Doctrine of signatures –

resemblance of a plant to the body part or the disease that it cures.
· Energetics – the properties of something in terms of its physical, emotional and psycho-spiritual energy.
· Fermentation – putrefaction of conjunction (*see* conjunction); metabolic process producing chemical changes through action of enzymes (such as yeast converting sugar into alcohol).
· Fixation – transformation of a volatile liquid into a stable solid.
· Hermetic seal – an airtight seal.
· Incineration – reduce a solution to fine, white ash.
· Multiplication – to multiply an alchemical formula.
· Nigredo – the blackening stage of calcination and dissolution.
· Philosophical month – 40 days, symbolic period of purification and renewal.
· Philosopher's stone – elixir of life and transformation.
· *Prima materia* – first matter, from which all else is formed.
· Projection – turn lead into gold using the philosopher's stone.
· Rubedo – the reddening stage of distillation and coagulation.
· Separation – filtration of a solution.
· Seven operations – also known as the seven rays, the seven primary alchemical processes (calcination, dissolution, separation, conjunction, fermentation, distillation, coagulation).
· Spagyric – the extraction of the life force from plants, coined by Paracelsus from the Greek *spao* (to tear apart) and *ageiro* (to gather together).
· *Tria prima* – the three essentials of alchemical sulphur, mercury and salt.
· *Vesica piscis* – sacred geometry; two intersecting circles of the same radius forming a lens in the centre.

ASTROLOGICAL TERMS

· Ascendant – the zodiac sign that was rising on the eastern horizon at the time of a person's birth.
· Balsamic moon – the waning crescent moon in the three days before the new moon, when the moon is less than 45 degrees behind the sun.
· Detriment (zodiac) – planetary placement where a planet is positioned in the opposite sign to the zodiac sign it rules, here it is challenged or debilitated. Also known as 'exile', it is the opposite of domicile.
· Domicile (zodiac) – planetary placement where a planet is positioned 'at home' in the zodiac sign it rules, here it is at ease.
· Esoteric ruler – higher soul expression of planetary rulerships of zodiac sign.
· Exalted (zodiac) – planetary placement where a planet is in a sign of the zodiac where it can express its full potential.
· Exoteric ruler – traditional or mundane planetary rulership of zodiac sign.
· In fall (zodiac) - planetary placement where a planet is in a sign of the zodiac that is opposite to its exaltation, where its functionality is weakened.
· Luminaries – the sun and the moon.
· Lunar phase – eight phases of a lunation: new moon, waxing crescent, first quarter, waxing gibbous, full moon, waning gibbous, third quarter and waning crescent.
· Lunation – a lunar month; the time it takes the moon to move from new moon to new moon (29.5 days).
· Modalities – conditions of expression, or modes of operation, of the zodiac signs: cardinal (initiates), fixed (preserves),

mutable (transforms).
· Planetary rulers – each sign has a relationship with a particular zodiac sign it is said to 'govern'.
· Planetary transit – when one celestial body passes in front of another, when a planet passes a zodiac sign in an astrological chart.
· Retrograde – when a planet appears to be going backwards in the sky.
· Rising sign – (*see* ascendant).
· Stellium – a cluster of several planets in a single zodiac sign or house in an astrological chart.
· Waning – between the full moon and new moon, when the moon's illumination is decreasing.
· Waxing – between the new moon and full moon, when the moon's illumination is increasing.

BOTANICAL TERMS

· Aerial parts – above-ground parts of the plant (leaves, flowers, stems) excluding roots.
· Annual – a plant that completes its life cycle in one year.
· Biennial – a plant that completes its life cycle in two years.
· Herbarium – a systemically arranged collection of dried plant samples for identification and research purposes.
· *Materia medica* – pharmacopoeia of medicinal plants and their actions on the body.
· Ovary –female reproductive organ of a flower, produces ovules.
· Perennial – a plant that lives for many years.
· Perianth – non-reproductive parts of a flower: petals and floral leaves.
· Stamen – male reproductive organ of a flower, produces pollen.
· Whole plant – All parts of the plant, above and below ground.

BOTANICAL PROPERTIES AND THERAPEUTIC ACTIONS

· Adaptogen – helps the body to adapt to stress and increases resilience to disease.
· Alterative – alters existing nutritive and excretory processes, cleanses the blood and restores normal body function.
· Analgesic – reduces or relieves pain.
· Anodyne – (*see* analgesic).
· Antifungal – inhibits fungal growth and prevents infection.
· Anti-inflammatory – reduces inflammation.
· Antioxidant – inhibits oxidative stress from free radicals that cause damage to cells and tissues.
· Antiparasitic – neutralises and eliminates parasites.
· Antiseptic – inhibits growth of microorganisms such as bacteria and viruses and counteracts putrefaction.
· Antispasmodic – reduces or prevents involuntary muscular contractions.
· Antiviral – inhibits or prevents viral infections.
· Aphrodisiac – stimulates sexual desire, increases pleasure performance.
· Aromatic – containing volatile oils with a strong smell, often used for digestive support.
· Astringent – tightens tissues and reduces secretions.
· Bitter – bitter taste that stimulates digestive juices.
· Cardiotonic – increase the tone and efficiency of heart muscle.
· Carminative – aids digestion and prevents or relieves gas.
· Demulcent – soothing and protective to inflamed tissues, due to mucilaginous properties.
· Diaphoretic – promotes sweating, to reduce fever and eliminate waste through the pores.
· Digestive – supports the normal function of the digestive system.
· Diuretic – promotes secretion and flow of urine.
· Elimination – removal of by-products and wastes in the body, known as excreta (faeces or urine).
· Emollient – soothing, hydrating and protective to the skin.
· Entheogen – psychoactive substance that generates an altered state of consciousness.
· Expectorant – promotes and facilitates the expulsion of mucus and catarrh from the respiratory system.
· Febrifuge – reduces fever.
· Galactogogue – increases milk secretion.
· Lymphagogue – promotes lymph production and flow through the lymphatic system.
· Lymphatic – supports lymphatic function and aids detoxification.
· Mucilage – polysaccharides with a gelatinous and viscous consistency (*see* demulcent).
· Narcotic – relieves pain, dulls the senses and induces sleep.
· Nervine –nerve tonic; nourishes and supports the nervous system.
· Nutritive – provides nourishment.
· Pathogen – microorganism that causes disease, such as a virus or bacterium.
· Purgative – activates and empties the bowels.
· Refrigerant – cooling, lowers body temperature.
· Rubefacient – increases local blood flow causing reddening to the skin.
· Sedative – relaxes the nervous system, lowers functional activity and encourages sleep.
· Soporific – induces a relaxing sleep.
· Stimulant – increases functional activity and energy in the body.
· Sudorific – relating to, or causing, sweating.
· Tonify – to give structure and tone to tissues (*see* tonic).
· Vulnerary – promotes the healing of wounds.

REMEDIES

· Aperitif – a drink, usually drunk before a meal, to aid digestion.
· Balm – a semi-solid ointment combining herb-infused oil.
· Compress – a cloth soaked in hot or cold herbal infusion or decoction and held on the affected area.
· Cordial – a remedy, often syrup-based, that is invigorating and stimulating.
· Crystal essence – vibrational essence made by imprinting the frequency of a crystal into water.
· Decoction – an extract made by simmering dense plant material (such as bark, rhizomes, roots or seeds) in water.
· Digestif – a drink, usually drunk after a meal, to aid digestion.
· Electuary – blend of herbs, usually in powder form, mixed into a paste with honey or syrup.
· Elixir – a liquid remedy for longevity.
· Extract – preparation made using a solvent to extract the beneficial components of a plant.
· Flower essence – vibrational essence made by imprinting the frequency of a flower into water.
· Fluid condenser – a liquid remedy that contains gold.
· Glycerite – a herbal preparation using vegetable glycerine.
· Homeopathic remedy – highly diluted substances prepared to trigger the body's own healing mechanisms.
· Hydrosol – water-based product of the distillation of plant matter.
· Infusions – an extract made by pouring water or oil over fresh or dried plant material.
· Maceration – extraction method whereby chopped or ground herbs placed in solvent for an extended period of time.
· Marc – the plant material used in making a herbal preparation.
· Mead – alcoholic drink made from fermented honey and water.
· Menstruum – a natural solvent, such as alcohol, used to extract compounds from plant material.
· Moon water – a liquid remedy infused with lunar rays.
· Oxymel – a remedy combining herb-infused vinegar with honey.
· Pastille – a rolled ball of sweet paste.
· Percolation – an extract made by placing ground, dried herbs in a percolator cone, covered in solvent.
· Poultice – a topical application of a soft, moist mass of plant material sometimes wrapped in muslin.
· Shrub – a drink made with vinegar, fruit and honey or sugar.
· Smokestick – a bundle of dried herbs burnt to cleanse a space.
· Solvent – liquid (water or alcohol) used to extract properties from a plant.
· Sun water – a liquid remedy infused with solar rays.
· Tincture – an extract of a plant made by soaking (macerating) herbs in an alcoholic solution.
· Tonic – restores, strengthens and supports organs and systems in the body.

Plant Directory

AGRIMONY (*Agrimonia eupatoria*)
FAMILY: *Rosaceae*
PARTS USED: Flowering tops
HARVEST: Late spring–early summer.

ANGELICA (*Angelica archangelica*)
FAMILY: *Apiaceae*
PARTS USED: Leaves, stems, flowers, root, seeds [Phototoxic compounds, furanocoumarins, may cause sun sensitivity]
HARVEST: Leaves in spring–summer of first year. Stems in spring of second year. Roots in autumn of first year or early spring of second. Seeds after flowering in second year.

BILBERRY (*Vaccinium myrtillus*)
FAMILY: *Ericaceae*
PARTS USED: Fruit, leaves
HARVEST: Berries in late summer–early autumn, when dark purple. Green leaves in early autumn.

BLACKBERRY (*Rubus fruticosus*)
FAMILY: *Rosaceae*
PARTS USED: Fruit, leaves, flowers, bark
HARVEST: Leaves before flowering. Berries in mid–late summer, when dark purple–black. Bark in spring.

BLADDERWRACK (*Fucus vesiculosus*)
FAMILY: *Fucaceae*
PARTS USED: Main stem (thallus)
HARVEST: Spring and early summer.

BORAGE (*Borago officinalis*)
FAMILY: *Boraginaceae*
PARTS USED: Flowers, blue parts only [Green parts contain toxic pyrrolizidine alkaloids]
HARVEST: Flowers in early summer, as opening.

CALENDULA (*Calendula officinalis*)
FAMILY: *Asteraceae*
PARTS USED: Flowers, leaves
HARVEST: Late spring–early autumn.

CHICORY (*Cichorium intybus*)
FAMILY: *Asteraceae*
PARTS USED: Flowers, leaves, roots
HARVEST: Leaves in early spring, flowers when in flower, roots autumn to spring.

CLEAVERS (*Galium aparine*)
FAMILY: *Rubiaceae*
PARTS USED: Leaves, stems, seeds
HARVEST: Early spring–summer, before flowering. Seeds late summer–autumn.

COMFREY (*Symphytum officinale*)
FAMILY: *Boraginaceae*
PARTS USED: Leaves, rhizome, roots [External use only due to pyrrolizidine alkaloids]
HARVEST: Leaves in late summer. Rhizome and roots in autumn–winter.

COMMON LIME (*Tilia × europaea*)
FAMILY: *Malvaceae*
PARTS USED: Flowers, leaves
HARVEST: Young leaves in spring. Flowers in summer, as opening.

CORNFLOWER (*Centaurea cyanus*)
FAMILY: *Asteraceae*
PARTS USED: Fruits, flowers, leaves
HARVEST: Flowers in spring, leaves in summer, fruits in autumn.

DAISY (*Bellis perennis*)
FAMILY: *Asteraceae*
PARTS USED: Leaves, flowers, roots
HARVEST: Leaves and flowers in spring–autumn. Roots in autumn.

DANDELION (*Taraxacum officinale*)
FAMILY: *Asteraceae*
PARTS USED: Leaves, flowers, roots
HARVEST: Young leaves and flowers in spring (also summer, although bitter). Roots autumn of second or third year.

DOG ROSE (*Rosa canina*)
FAMILY: *Rosaceae*
PARTS USED: Flowers, hips
HARVEST: Flowers in summer. Hips in autumn, ideally after first frost.

DOUGLAS FIR (*Pseudotsuga menziesii*)
FAMILY: *Pinaceae*
PARTS USED: Green tips, needles [Not to be confused with yew, which is poisonous. Needles should give off a citrus scent when crushed]
HARVEST: Green tips in spring–summer, when tender, but mature needles year-round.

ELDER (*Sambucus nigra*)
FAMILY: *Viburnaceae*
PARTS USED: Fruit, flowers [Leaves, bark and raw berries are toxic]
HARVEST: Flowers in late spring–early summer. Berries, mid–late summer, when deep purple.

FENNEL (*Foeniculum vulgare*)
FAMILY: *Apiaceae*
PARTS USED: Flowers, seeds, roots
HARVEST: Leaves in spring–autumn. Flowers in mid–late summer. Seeds in late summer, when ripe and green. Roots in autumn.

FIELD HORSETAIL (*Equisetum arvense*)
FAMILY: *Equisetaceae*
PARTS USED: Stems (aerial parts) [Not for prolonged use due to mildly toxic alkaloids]
HARVEST: Early summer. Cut stems well above ground.

FIELD POPPY (*Papaver rhoeas*)
FAMILY: *Papaveraceae*
PARTS USED: Flowers, leaves, seeds
HARVEST: Leaves from spring, before buds form. Flowers in summer. Seeds when rattling in pod.

GINKGO (*Ginkgo biloba*)
FAMILY: *Ginkgoaceae*
PARTS USED: Leaves [In moderation as contain ginkgotoxin, which can be toxic in high doses. Fruit and seeds contain toxic compounds that are not destroyed by heat]
HARVEST: Leaves in summer, while green.

GREAT MULLEIN (*Verbascum thapsus*)
FAMILY: *Scrophulariaceae*
PARTS USED: Leaves, flowers, occasionally root
HARVEST: Leaves after first year growth. Flowers in summer of second year. Roots in autumn of first year–early spring of second.

GROUND IVY (*Glechoma hederacea*)
FAMILY: *Lamiaceae*
PARTS USED: Leaves, flowers [Not to be confused with common ivy, or other species from the Araliaceae family which can be toxic]
HARVEST: Spring–early autumn.

GUELDER ROSE (*Viburnum opulus*)
FAMILY: *Viburnaceae*
PARTS USED: Fruit, bark [Leaves and raw berries toxic]
HARVEST: Berries in late summer–autumn. Bark in early spring, before leaves, or autumn, before leaves change colour.

HAWTHORN (*Crataegus monogyna*)
FAMILY: *Rosaceae*
PARTS USED: Leaves, flowers, fruit
HARVEST: Leaves in early–mid spring. Flowers in mid–late spring. BERRIES (haws) in late autumn, when ripe.

HONEYSUCKLE (*Lonicera periclymenum*)
FAMILY: *Caprifoliaceae*
PARTS USED: Flowers [Leaves and berries toxic]
HARVEST: Summer.

HORSERADISH (*Armoracia rusticana*)
FAMILY: *Brassicaceae*
PARTS USED: Roots, leaves
HARVEST: Leaves in spring–summer.
Roots in late autumn.

LADY'S MANTLE (*Alchemilla vulgaris*)
FAMILY: *Rosaceae*
PARTS USED: Leaves, stems,
flowers, root
HARVEST: Leaves and stems late
spring–early summer. Flowers in
summer. Roots in autumn. Whole
plant when in flower.

LAVENDER (*Lavandula angustifolia*)
FAMILY: *Lamiaceae*
PARTS USED: Flowers
HARVEST: Early spring–mid summer.

LEMON BALM (*Melissa officinalis*)
FAMILY: *Lamiaceae*
PARTS USED: Leaves
HARVEST: Spring, ideally just before
flowering, but throughout summer.

MALLOW (*Malva sylvestris*)
FAMILY: *Malvaceae*
PARTS USED: Flowers, leaves, root
HARVEST: Leaves in spring. Flowers
in summer. Root in autumn.

MEADOWSWEET (*Filipendula ulmaria*)
FAMILY: *Rosaceae*
PARTS USED: Flowers, leaves, root
HARVEST: Leaves in spring, before
flowering. Flowers in summer. Roots
in autumn.

MUGWORT (*Artemisia vulgaris*)
FAMILY: *Asteraceae*
PARTS USED: Leaves, flowers,
occasionally root
HARVEST: Leaves and stems in late
spring. Flowering stems in late
summer. Root in autumn.

PINEAPPLEWEED
(*Matricaria discoidea*)
FAMILY: *Asteraceae*
PARTS USED: Flowers
HARVEST: Late spring–early autumn.

RED CLOVER (*Trifolium pratense*)
FAMILY: *Fabaceae*
PARTS USED: Flowers
HARVEST: First blooms in late
spring–early summer.

SEA BUCKTHORN
(*Hippophae rhamnoides*)
FAMILY: *Elaeagnaceae*
PARTS USED: Fruit
HARVEST: Berries in late
summer–autumn.

SELF-HEAL (*Prunella vulgaris*)
FAMILY: *Lamiaceae*
PARTS USED: Flowers
HARVEST: Mid–late summer.

SILVER BIRCH (*Betula pendula*)
FAMILY: *Betulaceae*
PARTS USED: Leaves, bark, twigs,
pollen catkins, sap
HARVEST: Sap in early spring. Leaves
and bark in late spring.

SLOE, BLACKTHORN (*Prunus spinosa*)
FAMILY: *Rosaceae*
PARTS USED: Fruits, flowers, leaves
HARVEST: Flowers in spring, leaves
in summer, fruits in autumn.

STINGING NETTLE (*Urtica dioica*)
FAMILY: *Urticaceae*
PARTS USED: Leaves, seeds,
rhizomes, roots
HARVEST: Young leaves in early
spring or late summer–autumn.
Seeds in late summer. Rhizomes
and root in autumn. Whole plant
in spring.

ST JOHN'S WORT
(*Hypericum perforatum*)
FAMILY: *Hypericaceae*
PARTS USED: Flowers [Hypericin
may cause phototoxicity]
HARVEST: Summer.

SWEET VIOLET (*Viola odorata*)
FAMILY: *Violaceae*
PARTS USED: Leaves, flowers
HARVEST: Spring.

THYME (*Thymus vulgaris*)
FAMILY: *Lamiaceae*
PARTS USED: Leaves, stems, flowers
HARVEST: Year-round, ideally
early summer.

TURKEY TAIL (*Trametes versicolor*)
FAMILY: *Fucaceae* (Fungi)
PARTS USED: Fruiting body
HARVEST: Autumn, early winter.

WOOD BETONY (*Betonica officinalis*)
FAMILY: *Lamiaceae*
PARTS USED: Leaves, flowers
HARVEST: Spring–early summer,
before flowers fully open.

YARROW (*Achillea millefolium*)
FAMILY: *Asteraceae*
PARTS USED: Flowers, leaves, root
HARVEST: Flowers in summer–early
autumn. Leaves year-round. Root
in autumn.

'Nature itself is the
best physician.'
HIPPOCRATES

Index

Bibliography

Albertus, Frater, *Alchemist's Handbook*, Weiser, 1974

Atwood, Mary Ann. *A Suggestive Inquiry into Hermetic Mystery*, CreateSpace 2016

Baigent, Michael and Leigh, Richard, *The Elixir and The Stone, A History of Magic and Alchemy*, Viking, 1997

Barnard, Julian, *Bach Flower Remedies*, Lindisfarne, 2002

Bartlett, Robert A., *The Temper of Herbs*, Revelore Press, 2020

Begat, Odessa, *The Language of Flowers*, Harper Collins 2020

Beryl, Paul, *The Master Book of Herbalism*, Phoenix Publishing, 1984

Bevan, Rebecca, *The National Trust School of Gardening*, Pavilion Books, 2021

Blavatsky, Helena P., *Isis Unveiled*, Quest Books, 1997

Buhner, Stephen Harrod, *The Lost Language of Plants*, Chelsea Green Publishing, 2002

Burton-Seal, Julie and Seal, Matthew, *Hedgerow Medicine: Harvest and Make Your Own Herbal Remedies*, Merlin Unwin, 2008

Burton-Seal, Julie and Seal, Mattthew, *The Herbalist's Bible*, Merlin Unwin, 2014

Buttala, Lee and Siegel, Shanyn, *The Seed Garden: The Art and Practice of Seed Saving*, Chelsea Green, 2001

Campbell, Joseph, *The Inner Reaches of Outer Space*, New World, 1986

Coccia, Emanuele, *The Life of Plants: A Metaphysics of Mixture*, Polity Press, 2019

Critchlow, Keith, *The Hidden Geometry of Flowers*, Floris Books, 2011

Culpeper, Nicholas, *Complete Herbal*, Arcturus Publishing, 2019

Darrell, Nikki, *Conversations With Plants, Finding Ourselves In Nature Volume 1 and 2*, Veriditas Hibernica, 2014

De Cleene, Marcel and Lejeune, Marie Claire, *Compendium of Symbolic and Ritual Plants in Europe, Vol. I and II*, Man & Culture, 2003

Easley, Thomas and Horne, Steven, *The Modern Herbal Dispensatory: A Medicine-Making Guide*, North Atlantic, 2016

Edwards, Lawrence, *The Vortex of life: Nature's Patterns in Space and Time*, Floris Books, 2018

Eyre, Mike, *Harmonics of the Spheres: Towards a Unified Understanding of Astrology*, Ruby Star Press, 2020

Fritjof and Luisi, *The Systems View of Life: A Unifying Vision*, Cambridge University Press, 2016

Gagliano, Monica, *Thus Spoke the Plant*, North Atlantic, 2018

Gagliano, Monica, et al. *The Language of Plants*, Minnesota Press, 2017

Gooley, Tristan. *Wild Signs and Star Paths*, Sceptre, 2018

Green, James, *The Herbal Medicine-Makers Handbook*, Crossing Press, 2000

Griggs, Barbara, *The Green Pharmacy*, Jill Norman & Hobhouse 1981

Hall, Manly P. *The Secret Teachings of All Ages*. Jeremy P. Tarcher/Penguin, 2003

Hall, Manly P. et al. *A Collection of Writings Related to Occult, Esoteric, Rosicrucian and Hermetic Literature, Including Freemasonry, the Kabbalah, the Tarot, Alchemy and Theosophy* Volumes 1–4. Lamp of Trismegistus, 2019

Hall, Matthew, *Plants as Persons: A Philosophical Botany*, Suny Press, 2011

Hand, Robert, *Planets in Transit, Life Cycles for Living*, Schiffer, 2001

Harford, Robin, *Edible and Medicinal Wild Plants of Britain and Ireland*, Eatweeds, 2019

Hartmann, Franz, *Alchemy and Astrology*, 2005

Hatfield, Gabrielle, *Hatfield's Herbal*, Penguin, 2007

Hauk, Dennis William, *Laboratory Alchemy*, Create Space, *2017*

Hauk, Dennis William, *Spagyric Alchemy*, Create Space, *2017*

Hoffman, David, *Holistic Herbal*, Element Books, 1988

Hoffman, David, *Medical Herbalism*, Healing Arts , 2003

Hughes, Nathaniel and Owen, Fiona, *Weeds in the Heart*, Quintessence Press, 2016

Johnson & Smith, *Plant Names Simplified*, Old Pond Publishing, 2008

Johnson, Owen and More, David, *Tree Guide, The Most Complete Field Guide to the Trees of Britain and Europe*, Harper Collins, 2004

Jung, Carl G, *Psychology and alchemy*, Routledge, 1980

Jung, Carl G, *Man and His Symbols*, Dell Publishing, 1964

Klossowski De Rola, Stanislas, *The Arcane Doctrine of Alchemy*, Thames & Hudson, 2013

Kranich, Ernst Michael, *Planetary Influences Upon Plants, A Cosmological Botany*, Bio-Dynamic Association, 1986

Levi, Eliphas, *The History of Magic*, A Yesterday's World, 2019

Lipton, Bruce, *The Biology of Belief*, Hay House, 2055

Mancuso, Stefano, *The Revolutionary Genius of Plants: A New Understanding of Plant Intelligence and Behaviour*, 2017

Marder, Michael, *Plant Thinking: A Philosophy of Vegetal Life*, Colombia University Press, 2013

Masson, Pierre. *A Biodynamic Manual*, Floris Books, 2014

Maveric Jean, *Hermetic Herbalism: The Art of Extracting Spagyric Essences*. Inner Traditions, 2020

Naydler, Jeremy, *Goethe on Science*, Floris Books, 1996

North, Chris and Abel, Paul, *How to Read the Solar System*, BBC Books, 2013

Pengelly, Andrew, *The Constituents of Medicinal Plants*, CABI, 2021

Phillips, Roger, *Wild Food*, Pan Books, 1983

Popham, Sajah, *Evolutionary Herbalism: Science, Spirituality and Medicine from the Heart of Nature*, North Atlantic Books, 2019

Raff, Jeffrey, *Jung and The Alchemical Imagination*, Nicolas-Hays, 2000

RHS, *Complete Gardener's Manual*, DK, 2020

RHS, *RHS Botany for Gardeners: The Art and Science of Gardening Explained and Explored*, Octopus, 2013

Schultz, Joachim, *The Movement and Rhythms of the Stars*, Floris Books, 2008

Silberer, Herbert, *Hidden Symbolism of Alchemy and The Occult Arts*, Dover, 1971

Sinnot, Edmund W., *Cell and Psyche: The Biology of Purpose*, Harper Torchbook, 1961

Spence, Ian, *Gardening Through the Year*, DK, 2018

Stamets, Paul, *Mycelium Running: How Mushrooms Can Help Save the World*, Penguin, 2005

Stearn, T. William, *Botanical Latin*, Timber Press, 1966

Steiner, Rudolf, *Agriculture Course. The Birth of the Biodynamic Method*. Rudolf Steiner Press, 2004

Sterry, Paul and Hughes, Barry, *Complete Guide to British Mushrooms and Toadstools*, Collins, 2009

Strehlow, Dr Wighard and Hertzka, Gottfried, *Hildegard of Bingen's Medicine*, Bear & Company, 1988

Streeter, David, Hart-Davies, C., Hardcastle, A., Cole, F. and Harper, L., *Wild Flower Guide*, Collins, 2016

Tarnas Richard, *Cosmos and Psyche*, Plume, 2006

Three Initiates, *The Kybalion – Centenary Edition: Hermetic Philosophy*, Tarcher Perigee, 2018

Topalovic, Radmila and Kerss Tom, *Stargazing, Beginners Guide to Astronomy*, Collins, 2009

Vreede, Elisabeth, *Astronomy and Spiritual Science*. SteinerBooks, 2007

Warm, Hartmut, *Signature of the Celestial Spheres: Discovering Order in the Solar System*, Sophia Books, 2010

Wood, Matthew, *The Earthwise Herbal Repertory*, North Atlantic 2016

Wood, Matthew, *Seven Herbs: Plants as Teachers*, North Atlantic 1986

Worwood, Valerie Anna. *The Fragrant Pharmacy*. Bantam 1991

Picture Credits

With thanks to the following illustrators for their contribution to this book:
Andreas Brooks – front cover (based on plant drawing by Patrick Guenette/Alamy Stock Photo). – pp.10–11, 22–23, 32–33, 52–53, 56, 60, 64, 68, 72, 78, 82, 86, 90, 94, 98, 102, 106, 110, 114, 118, 124, 128, 132, 136, 140, 144, 148, 152, 156, 160, 164, 168, 172–73.
Raxenne Maniquiz – pp.4, 9, 26–27, 29, 34–35, 37, 40, 42, 48–49, 58, 62, 66, 70, 74, 80, 84, 88, 92, 96, 100, 104, 108, 120, 126, 130, 134, 138, 142, 146, 150, 154, 158, 162, 166, 170, 174, 177, 183, 192.

The publisher would also like to thank the copyright holders for granting permission to reproduce works illustrated in this book. Every effort has been made to contact the holders of copyright material, and any omission will be corrected in future editions if the publisher is notified in writing.
P.13 – Logic Images/Alamy Stock Photo.
P.14 – Wellcome Collection 38820i.
P.16 – Science History Images/Alamy Stock Photo.
P.19 – Charles Walker Collection/Alamy Stock Photo.
P.112 – Getty Images/bauhaus1000.
P.116 – Getty Images/Florilegius.

Rosebay willowherb (*Epilobium angustifolium*).